THE CULT
of the
ALL-SEEING EYE

By

ROBERT KEITH SPENSER

The Christian Book
Club of America

ISBN: 978-2-925369-65-3
Printed in the USA.

THE NEW AGE

April, 1960
Volume LXVIII, Number 4

Masonic Symbols In a $1 Bill

13 leaves in the olive branches
13 bars and stripes in the shield
13 feathers in the tail
13 arrows
13 letters in the "E Pluribus Unum" on the ribbon
13 stars in the green crest above
32 long feathers representing the 32° in Masonry
13 granite stones in the Pyramid with the Masonic "All-seeing Eye" completing it.
13 letters in Annuit Coeptis, "God has prospered."

On the front of the dollar bill is the seal of the United States made up of a key, square, and the Scales of Justice, as well as a compass which, of course, is an important symbol in Masonry.

James B. Walker 32°

THE OFFICIAL ORGAN OF
THE SUPREME COUNCIL 33°
ANCIENT & ACCEPTED SCOTTISH RITE OF
FREEMASONRY SOUTHERN JURISDICTION
UNITED STATES OF AMERICA

1733 SIXTEENTH STREET, N. W.
WASHINGTON, D. C.

(See page 27, 4th paragraph)

TABLE OF CONTENTS

*Articles by Edith Kermit Roosevelt

LIST OF ILLUSTRATIONS

INTRODUCTION

The Cult of the All-Seeing Eye has existed under many names and guises for thousands of years. Through the ages its high priests have worshipped before unhallowed altars dedicated to the adoration of a nameless deity — an Unknown God. The identity of this deity has been concealed behind an elaborate system of veiled allegories and secret symbols. Followers of this pseudo-mystical, humanistic, occult system of beliefs affirm, without proof, that it is based on an unbroken oral tradition handed down from an ancient priesthood in Egypt.

The Cult projects a minimum belief in a god which totally excludes God, The Divine Redeemer, and which rejects Jesus Christ, the Son of God. Its leaders tell its initiates that the doctrine of the Cult is based on a *hidden master religion* in which all men can agree because it is founded on pre-Christian, pagan models that appear not to be in conflict with reputable faiths.

This offspring of the ancient idolatrous mystery cults has existed in America for centuries, but its leaders have never dared to admit that they hope to replace Christianity with the Cult. However, in recent years, they *have* dared to establish small, public temples in the United States: namely, the Meditation Rooms in the United Nations and at Wainwright House, Rye, New York, and the Prayer Room in the U.S. Capitol. Their great Temple of Understanding is soon to be erected in Washington, D.C.

The strange, fascinating history of the Great Seal of the United States was included in this study because the symbolism of the three Rooms and the Temple is centered around the All-Seeing Eye which appears on the reverse side of the Seal as depicted on the one dollar bill.

The Cult is seeking to obliterate the Christian ideal by attempting to destroy all honoured standards and traditions set up during the past nineteen centuries for the protection of the civilized world. The lure of famous names associated with the Cult has drawn many naive supporters into its fold who would recoil in horror from its evil teachings were the truth only known to them.

The secret doctrine of the Cult has been carefully guarded from public scrutiny and investigation. Nevertheless, this study cuts to the very heart of the meaning of that doctrine and the symbolism employed by the Cult. It uncovers the trail of the serpent. It arms Christians with the knowledge they *must* have if they are to detect and destroy this insidious menace which threatens the very foundation of Christian civilization.

PART I

The United Nations Meditation Room

The Meditation Room is 30 feet long, 18 wide at the entrance (which faces north north-east), and 9 wide at the other end. It is therefore wedge-shaped. Its only entrance is through two tinted glass-paned doors outside of which stands a U.N. guard. Inside the room is another guard. Once through the doors, the visitor finds himself in a darkened corridor which leads to the left. The sharp transition from a world of light to one of extreme darkness *forces* a feeling of abrupt withdrawal from the outside world upon the senses of the visitor who walks along the corridor, reaches the inner arched entrance, turns right, and looks into the room.

The room is very dimly lit. The only source of light, at first glance, is that which is reflected squarely from the gleaming upper surface of the brooding, somber altar in the center of the room. A special lens recessed in the ceiling focuses a beam of light on the altar from a point above and just beyond its far edge. Thin lines of bluish light lap the edges of the shadow cast by the altar.

The acoustical properties of the room are unique. The edges of padding material behind the paneling on the walls can be detected at the ceiling level. This absorbs sound as does the Swedish-woven blue rug which covers the floor of the corridor and the back of the room. The room is as quiet as an underground tomb. Its floor is paved with blue-gray slate slabs laid in a haphazard pattern. At the edge of the rug are two very low railings extending out from the east and west walls of the room. The center space between the railings is some six feet in width. To the right of the inner entrance are ten low wicker benches arranged in two rows of three and one back row of four against the corridor wall. Attempts by visitors to pass the railings are discouraged by the guard.

The mural is a fresco which was painted originally on wet plaster one section at a time by the artist with the aid of an expert in this work brought from Europe. It is set into a steel-framed narrow panel projected from the wall, behind which is an enclosed area some six inches deep which has its own light source. A small, square projector set close against the front base of the altar throws a diffused beam of light from a recessed aperture upon the surface of the mural. There are also ten hidden lights, five on each side of the room, behind the upper edges of a thin suspended ceiling which extends out over the room from the top of the mural. The 18 inch space between the two ceilings contains the light control apparatuses. The lower ceiling is wedge-shaped and separated from three walls of the inner room by a foot-wide space. Thus the room appears to be much longer than it really is because of the many converging lines leading into the narrow end, the corners of which are rounded off on either side of the mural.

THE ALTAR

The altar is four feet high and rests on two narrow cross pieces. It is a dark gray block of crystalline iron ore from a Swedish mine and weighs six and one-half tons. The Swedish Government presented this block of ore — the largest of its kind ever mined — to the U.N. in early 1957. "The chunk rests on a concrete pillar that goes straight down to bed-rock."[1] The area and passageway beneath the room are closed to the public.

The chunk of ore has been described as a lodestone, or magnetite, which is strongly magnetic and which possesses polarity. "In northern Sweden are what may be the largest magnetite deposits in the world, believed to have been formed by segregation in the magma."[2] Magma is the term for molten material held in solution under the pressure of the earth's crust.

THE MURAL

The fresco mural was described in the *UN Review* of January 1958 as having been designed "to conform with the purity of line and color sought, for what Secretary General Dag Hammarskjold has called 'a room of stillness'." It was painted predominately in shades of grays and blues but includes yellow and white patterns and a black half-sphere. Light pure colors intersect to form deeper shades. The *New York Times*[3] described the fresco as being eight feet eight inches in height and six feet eight inches in width; more brightly illuminated at the top than at the bottom.

Bo Beskow, an old friend of Dag Hammarskjold, painted the mural. "Dag had me start sketches on this last summer," he said. "He wanted me to do the actual work right here in the room, so I have been here since October 6 [1957]." The mural was seen for the first time on November 11, 1957. During the period of the remodeling the guards were on hand during the day to keep out the curious and at night the room was locked up with a chain and padlock. The artist said of his work, "It has no title, and *you can make what you wish of it.*"

He explained that the geometric patterns in the mural repeated the proportions of the room and those of the focal point of the room, the piece of iron ore. He also said that he intended to give a feeling of space with the picture. The *UN Review* story stated that "he sought to open up the room so that the eye can travel in the distance when it strikes the wall. To give a slight upward movement, he said he designed winding circles and a spiraling diagonal line which might be compared to a vibrating musical chord. As a 'resting spot' for the viewer's eyes, he provided one spot of black amid the light colors, a half circle *at which all lines of the fresco and the room converge.*"

In the *New Yorker* story cited earlier (see sources), Beskow was quoted as saying: "My fresco contained no intentional symbols, though I've heard people say that the black-and-pale-blue circle in the upper middle section of the panel stands for the cosmos. All that I seriously sought to do was *to open up the wall,* in order to let the eye travel farther, and to open up the mind, provoking meditation but not directing it." (All emphasis supplied.)

The mystic, P. D. Ouspensky, has written[4] that in "real art nothing is accidental. It is mathematics. Everything in it can be calculated, everything can be known beforehand. The artist *knows* and *understands* what he wants to convey and his work cannot produce one impression on one man and another impression on another, presuming, of course, [they are] people on one level. . . . At the same time the same work of art will produce different impressions on people of different levels. And people from lower levels will never receive from it what people of higher levels receive. This is real, *objective* art. . . . An objective work of art . . . affects the emotional and not only the intellectual side of man." (His emphasis.)

Mr. Beskow's picture is described as nonobjective, yet its composition admittedly reflects the dimensions of the room and the chunk of iron ore — this involves mathematics. He said of his mural, "you can make what you wish of it," yet he admittedly sought to create a specific subjective effect in the mind of the spectator. Consequently, Mr. Beskow's remarks create confusion rather than understanding.

'THE ROOM OF STILLNESS'

The leaflet made available to those who visit the Meditation Room was written under the direction of Dag Hammarskjold. Its description of the room is deliberately couched in abstruse language. It contains terms which have meaning to the esoterically inclined but not to the uninitiated. These terms will be explained in later sections of this study.

The leaflet reads: "We all have within us a center of stillness surrounded by silence. . . . People of many faiths will meet here, and for that reason none of the symbols to which we are accustomed in our meditation could be used.

"However, there are simple things which speak to us all with the same language. We have sought for such things and we believe that we have found them in the shaft of light striking the shimmering surface of solid rock.

"So, in the middle of the room we see a symbol of how, daily, the light of the skies gives life to the earth on which we stand, a symbol to many of us of how the light of the spirit gives life to matter.

"But the stone in the middle of the room has more to tell us. We may see it as an altar, empty not because there is no God, not because it is an altar to an unknown god, but because it is dedicated to the God whom man worships under many names and in many forms.

"The stone in the middle of the room reminds us also of the firm and permanent in a world of movement and change. The block of iron ore has the weight and solidity of the everlasting. It is a reminder of that cornerstone of endurance and faith on which all human endeavor must be based.

"The material of the stone leads our thoughts to the necessity for choice between destruction and peace. Of iron man has forged his swords, of iron he has also made his ploughshares. . . .

"The shaft of light strikes the stone in a room of utter simplicity. . . . When our eyes travel from these symbols to the front wall, they meet a simple pattern *opening up the room* to the harmony, freedom and balance of space.

"There is an ancient [Chinese] saying that the sense of a vessel is not in its shell but in the void. So it is with this room. It is for those who come here to fill the void with what they find in their center of stillness." (Emphasis supplied.)

LODESTONE

The World Goodwill Bulletin is published by Lucis Press Ltd. (owned by Lucis Trust) at 88 Edgware Rd., Marble Arch, London W-2, England. The New York branch, the Lucis Publishing Company (11 W. 42nd St., 32nd floor), issues materials on its Arcane School, three-member Triangles, and World Service Fund, and publishes the *Beacon Magazine*. This company was originally established as the Lucifer Publishing Co., but changed its name on Nov. 11, 1924 to the less startling one it bears today. A third branch of the Lucis Trust is located at 1 Rue de Varembe(3E), Geneva, Switzerland. Alice A. Bailey, the now deceased High Priestess of the occult Arcane School, established and headed the Trust and its self-identified Society of Illumined Minds. This powerful group has intimate connections with the United Nations.

The World Goodwill Bulletin issued a special edition on the United Nations in July, 1957, which contained an article entitled "Lodestone." We quote from its description of the Meditation Room: "The visitor will be totally unprepared for what he will see as he steps in the door for a moment of quiet. . . . Because of the converging walls and the dim light, *he will experience a peculiar spatial disorientation,* and dimension and perspective will seem difficult to establish. In the center of the room, he will see, illuminated by a single point of light from the ceiling, a rectangular mass. . . .

"The ore piece . . . is many millions of years old . . . one feels . . . as though one is in a repository for some *natural talisman of significant and noble importance* rather than in a chapel in the ordinary sense. . . . Those who are wedded to seeking communion in traditional settings may be somewhat ill at ease here. This is a sudden break with prior experience. One is thrown violently upon his [own] resources.

"The room and the concept do not seem indicative of the supplications or the dualistic concept of the mystic in which illumination is sought as a boon granted by Deity. Rather, seemingly inherent in the decoration of the room, in the pinpoint of light playing on the ore, is the concept of a personal concentration of forces, creating a focus that illumines the field of attention. . . .

"The pinpoint of light, the void of space, the illuminated crystalline ore — one feels projected into a setting of cosmological symbolism rather than one of planetary or even solar intent.

"It is interesting to speculate on what *the long-term influence of this 'new departure' will be on current religious thinking.* Ensconced here in the highest Hall Of Man, it cannot be inconsiderable. Whatever interpretations one may attribute to the United Nations Meditation Room, it can be said with certainty that the words and the repercussions have only just begun." (Emphasis supplied.)

The 'new departure' in religion referred to did not occur by chance. Tremendous pressure was brought to bear on Trygve Lie and Dag Hammarskjold to install such a room at the U.N. by such organizations as the World Council of Churches.[5] Trygve Lie announced on April 18, 1949, that such a room would be established.[6] The 5th General Assembly opened with one minute of silence as a "religious" observance. Shortly thereafter a temporary meditation room was provided at Lake Success, N. Y. On February 9, 1951, a meditation room was opened for one day at the U.N. Secretariat building. On October 14, 1952, the opening day of the 7th General Assembly, a permanent Meditation Room was made available to the public. Since then each Assembly has opened with one minute of silence.

In 1955[7] the Meditation Room contained a 300-year old, 800-pound, 37-inch wide upright section of an agba (mahogany) tree from French Equatorial Africa. It was the idea of Wallace Harrison, director of the international board of architects which planned the U.N.; co-architect and director of Rockefeller Center; and member of the board of directors of the socialist New School of Social Research in New York City (See *Who's Who* In America, 1959.) The room contained a philodendron plant on the altar, to symbolize some unknown person killed in a war; an olive green rug; 25 russet-colored chairs; and a blue and white U.N. banner set in front of a ceiling-to-floor white drape.

FRIENDS OF THE MEDITATION ROOM

On February 16, 1953, a group known as the Friends of the Meditation Room, numbering 1500 members, presented through its officers a set of guest books to the U.N. wherein visitors to the room could inscribe their names, addresses, and religious affiliations. *Three and one-half to four million* visitors have been estimated by the U.N. to have entered the room from October 14, 1952 to June 1963. Over 750,000 of these visitors have signed 108 of these books, each containing 7,000 names.

What purpose is served by the accumulation of these thousands of names of individuals, with their religious affiliations, who visit the room and who — by the act of signing their names — indicate that they do *not* object to the existence of this pagan temple?

The Friends are a product of the "non-sectarian" Laymen's Movement for a Christian World, Inc., the international headquarters of which is located at Wainwright House, Milton Point, Rye, New York. Warren R. Austin, a past permanent U.S. delegate to the U.N., headed a Friend's committee which presented $12,600 to Hammarskjold on April 24, 1957, as first payment on $25,000 needed to remodel and enlarge the room.[8]

The Movement has issued "U.N. Meditation Room Identification Cards [to] 300 men and women who go periodically to this room for prayer." (See *UN Room,* by this group.) It once issued Prayer Cards to visitors containing Prayers from the "World's Great Living Religions," namely, Hinduism, Buddhism, Judaism, Islamism, Sikhism, Christianity and St. Francis of Assisi(!). The Friends held Vigils of Prayer in the room in 1953 and 1954. Back in 1946 the Movement had sent Dr. Frank Laubach, Union Theological Seminary graduate and author of "Letters of a Modern Mystic," to the Paris Peace Conference to lobby for the establishment of the Meditation Room.

Speakers for the Movement's meetings have included Norman Cousins, Ralph Bunche and Frank P. Graham of the U.N., and William Ernest Hocking and Kirtley F. Mather of Harvard, all of whom have communist-front records (see May-June and July-August 1959 and July-August 1962 issues of *The Laymen's Movement Review*).

The Movement has included among its members Dwight D. Eisenhower (*Ibid.*, July-August 1961). The most important Friend of the Movement from its inception, however, has been John D. Rockefeller, Jr. A Methodist missionary, Weyman C. Huckabee, secured and received grants from John D. Rockefeller, Jr.'s Davison Fund and from his (New York City) Riverside Church funds for five consecutive years (1937-41), for a health center in Hiroshima, Japan (*Ibid.*, May-June 1960). Huckabee then became the secretary of the Movement in New York in 1941 and secured two grants a year for the organization from the Davison Fund until it was liquidated. Thereafter, Rockefeller continued his yearly grants without fail from his own personal funds. During the 22 years Huckabee remained with the Movement a million dollars was raised for its work (*Ibid.*, July-August 1962).

When the Movement first sought to secure Wainwright House for its headquarters in 1951, John D. Rockefeller, Jr., gave $5,000.00 of the $25,000.00 needed (*Ibid.*, May-June 1961). Since 1951, 10,000 individuals have signed the guest book at Wainwright House; 5,000 have attended its public meetings; its members have been addressed by the President of the National Council of Churches, J. Irwin Miller (*Ibid.*, May-June 1962); its conference rooms have been used by the Episcopal, Presbyterian, Methodist, Baptist, Congregationalist, and Quaker churches (*Ibid.*, January-February 1963).

When the Friends of the Meditation Room agreed to raise $15,000 to pay for the redecoration of the Room, John D. Rockefeller, Jr. gave $5,000 of the amount sought (*Ibid.*, May-June 1960). Dag Hammarskjold personally raised another $10,000 from the Marshall Field family for the cost of the fresco in the Room (*Ibid.*, November-December 1961). The United Steel Workers, CIO-AFL, gave $500.00 (*Ibid.*, July-August 1961).

The Movement was formed in 1940. The man who started it was Dr. Arthur Compton, the scientist who first brought the identified Communist and accused espionage agent, Professor J. Robert Oppenheimer, into the atomic energy project in 1942 (*Ibid.*, July-August 1961).

Wainwright House has its own Meditation Room, on its second floor. The room contains the agba wood altar first used in the U.N. Meditation Room, and the cherry wood chairs and drapes from that room, presented to the Friends by the U.N. in 1957 (*Ibid.*, November-December 1961). The House also contains a large library centered around the Thomas Sugrue Memorial Library, a sixteen hundred dollar collection of books on religion and occultism – where one may read up on spiritualism, Zen, Taoism, Yoga, Judaism, etc. Every book in the library has a bookplate therein designed by the artist, Fritz Eichenberg.

His bookplate "depicts the ancient cross in the shape of a T, surrounded by a serpent symbolizing wisdom and healing, and forming the letter S. The

T and S, Thomas Sugrue's initials, are crowned by the lotus, Vedantic representation of all being. In the background lies the city of Jerusalem over which shine two stars, the star of the East of Christianity and six-pointed star of Judaism. A flame spreads an arc of light above, proclaiming the continuity of life and the immortality of the soul." (*Ibid.*, March-April 1960, pp. 6-7.)

M. Oldfield Howey tells us in *The Encircled Serpent,* (David Mackay Co., Philadelphia, Pa., 192-, p. 84), that in the symbolism of Egypt the "serpent is constantly represented as surmounting a cross . . . the Brazen Serpent . . . was a palladium or talisman in the form of a serpent coiled around the mystic Tau, or T. [Also,] the serpent set up by Moses was originally the Egyptian . . . Sun-God, who was now known to his people as Jehovah." (*Ibid.*, p. 83.) Joseph von Hammer, in *The History of the Assassins* (Eng. trans., 1835) explains the tau as the figure of the phallus. (See also source 9, p. 791.)

"Among the Egyptians, the lotus was the symbol of Osiris and Isis. It was esteemed a sacred ornament by the priests." (*Ibid.*, p. 477.) The six-pointed star is the great Oriental talisman known as the Seal of Solomon. Its meaning and the identity of Osiris and Isis will be explained in Part II on the Great Seal of the United States. The arc of light on the bookplate is the En Soph, from the Cabalistic writings (mystical theosophy) which teach that it created the world by virtue of ten emanations from The Infinite One. The emanations, or Sephiroth, are arranged into a form called the Tree of Life, which in turn is vertically composed of three pillars. C. W. King, in his *Gnostics,* (p. 12.) states that the two outer pillars "figure largely amongst all the secret societies of modern times, and naturally so; for these illuminati have borrowed, without understanding it, the phraseology of the Cabalists." (*Ibid.*, pp. 390-391.)

THE CORNERSTONE

Dag Hammarskjold called the altar a reminder of that "cornerstone... on which all human endeavor must be based." The Meditation Room faces north north-east. To enter the room one must proceed from darkness to light. With these facts in mind note the cabalistic symbolism of the following description of the cornerstone by an authority:[9] "In its situation it lies between the north, the place of darkness, and the east, the place of light; and hence this position symbolizes ... progress *from darkness to light,* and from ignorance to knowledge. The permanence and durability of the corner-stone ... is intended [to remind us that long after our death we have within ourselves] a sure foundation of eternal life — a corner-stone of immortality — an emanation ... which pervades all nature, and which, therefore, must survive the tomb." (Emphasis supplied)

On a "higher" level of "esoteric knowledge" the metal altar or stone can be likened to the ancient Stone of Foundation, which, according to the same authority cited above, was supposed "to have been ... placed at one time within the foundations of the Temple of Solomon, and afterwards, during the building of the second Temple, transported to the Holy of Holies. It was in the form of a perfect cube, and had inscribed upon its upper face, within a delta or triangle, the sacred Tetragrammaton, or ineffable name of God."

In a "scurrilous book of the Middle Ages . . . the *Life of Jesus*" there was another account of the stone: "At that time there was in the Temple the ineffable name of God, inscribed upon the Stone of Foundation." This scandalous book proceeded to state that Our Saviour "cunningly obtained a knowledge of the Tetragrammaton from the Stone of Foundation, and by its mystical influence was enabled to perform his miracles [Cf.*Mark 3:22] . . . there was a very general prevalence among the earliest nations of antiquity of the worship of stones as the representative of Deity . . . in almost every ancient temple there was a legend of a sacred or mystical stone . . . the mystical stone there has received the name of the 'Stone of Foundation.' "[10] (*"And the Scribes who had come down from Jerusalem said, 'He has Beelzebub,' and, 'By the prince of devils he casts out devils.' ")

Alfred Edward Waite, in his study of the Zohar (the cabalistic textbook of the 14th century), entitled *The Secret Doctrine of Israel* (Occult Research Press, N. Y., 191-), wrote (p. 62) of "a mysterious stone called *Schethiya*" which was cast by Jehovah "into the abyss, so to form the basis of the world and give birth thereto. One might say otherwise that it was like a cubical stone or altar, for its extremity was concealed in the depth, while its surface or summit rose above the chaos. It was the central point in the immensity of the world, the cornerstone [*Zohar*, Pt. I, folio 231a; II, 511; Job xxxviii, *6*], the tried stone, the sure foundation, but also that stone which the builders rejected."

But what, really, in the Christian meaning, is the cornerstone? Isaias said (Isa. 28, verse 16): "Therefore thus saith the Lord God: Behold I will lay a stone in the foundations of Sion, a tried stone, a corner stone, a precious stone, founded in the foundation. He that believeth, let him not hasten." The corner stone is Jesus Christ, "the stone which the builders rejected." (Cf. Ps. 118, 22; Mt. 21, 42ff; Acts 4,11; Romans 9, 33; Eph. 2, 20; 1 Pe. 2, 6ff.)

One need go no further than the inner entrance of the Meditation Room to see concrete evidence of the Godlessness of the U.N. The "stone," the metal altar, in its stark setting in that Room is in itself a symbol of idolatry. "Stone worship was perhaps the earliest form of Fetichism. . . . Eussebius cites Porphyry as saying that the ancients represented the Deity by a black stone, because his nature is obscure and inscrutable. The reader here will be reminded of the black stone, *Hadsjar el Aswad*, placed in the south-west corner of the Kaaba at Mecca, which was worshipped by the ancient Arabians. . . . The Druids, it is well known, had no other images of their gods but cubical or sometimes columnar stones . . . to use the language of Dudley, the pillar or stone 'was adapted as a symbol of strength and firmness — a symbol, also, of the divine power, and, by a ready inference, *a symbol or idol of the Deity himself*.' . . . the god Hermes [Mercury] was represented without hands or feet, being a cubical stone, because the cubical figure betokened his solidity and stability."[11] (Emphasis supplied)

Hammarskjold, in the speech quoted earlier, said: "In this case we wanted this massive 'altar' to give the impression of something more than temporary. . . . We had another idea . . . we thought we could bless by our thoughts the very material out of which arms are made." The description of the altar as a "natural talisman" by the World Goodwill group also is significant. Talisman is a term which means a stone, or other object, engraven with figures or characters to which is attributed the occult powers of the planetary influences and celestial configurations under which it was made.

Altars, "among the ancients, were generally made of turf or stone... usually in a cubical form. Altars were erected long before temples."[12] The shaft of light upon the altar in the Meditation Room casts a shadow to the north. "The use of the north as a symbol of darkness (is)... a portion of the old sun worship, of which we find so many relics in Gnosticism, in Hermetic philosophy.... The east was the place of the sun's daily birth, and hence highly revered; the north the place of his annual death."[13]

Finally, it must be emphasized above all that the altar in the Meditation Room is unsanctified and unhallowed. It has no sacred meaning, can inspire no reverence, and is not inviolable. This altar cannot be used for sacrifice in any other than an unholy sense.

THE SECRET OF THE MURAL

One clue to the mural's symbolism is given in Hammarskjold's and Beskow's descriptions of its purpose. It was to "open up the wall," to give a feeling of space, of the void — in effect, to extend the room further out, into another dimension as it were. The Friends' leaflet, "A Call To Prayer," states the theme of the mural is "infinity."

Let us look at this mural squarely from the viewpoint of the esoterically inclined, the occultist. There is an asymmetrical arrangement of the entire mural into what is called a "Magic Square," which is a square arranged in an equal number of cells — in this case nine — three rows up and three rows down. The game tit-tat-toe is based on this type of square. The talismanic magic square has a series of numbers in the cells, "the enumeration of all of whose columns, vertically, horizontally, and diagonally, will give the same sum." The following nine digits[14] so arranged as to add up to 15 in any direction were regarded as sacred, because 15 is the numerical value of the Hebrew word for God, JAH, which is one of the forms of the Tetragrammaton:

4	9	2
3	5	7
8	1	6

The predominately dark blue rectangle which occupies most of the middle tier of the mural, the upper side of which passes through the exact middle of the small bisected sphere, represents the altar. The yellow rectangle set at an angle into the lower and middle tiers so that one corner touches the bottom of the mural is a second representation of the altar. They indicate duality: the yellow figure — light (sun); the blue figure — earth (altar). Both rectangular figures are overlaid in part by other patterns in other colors.

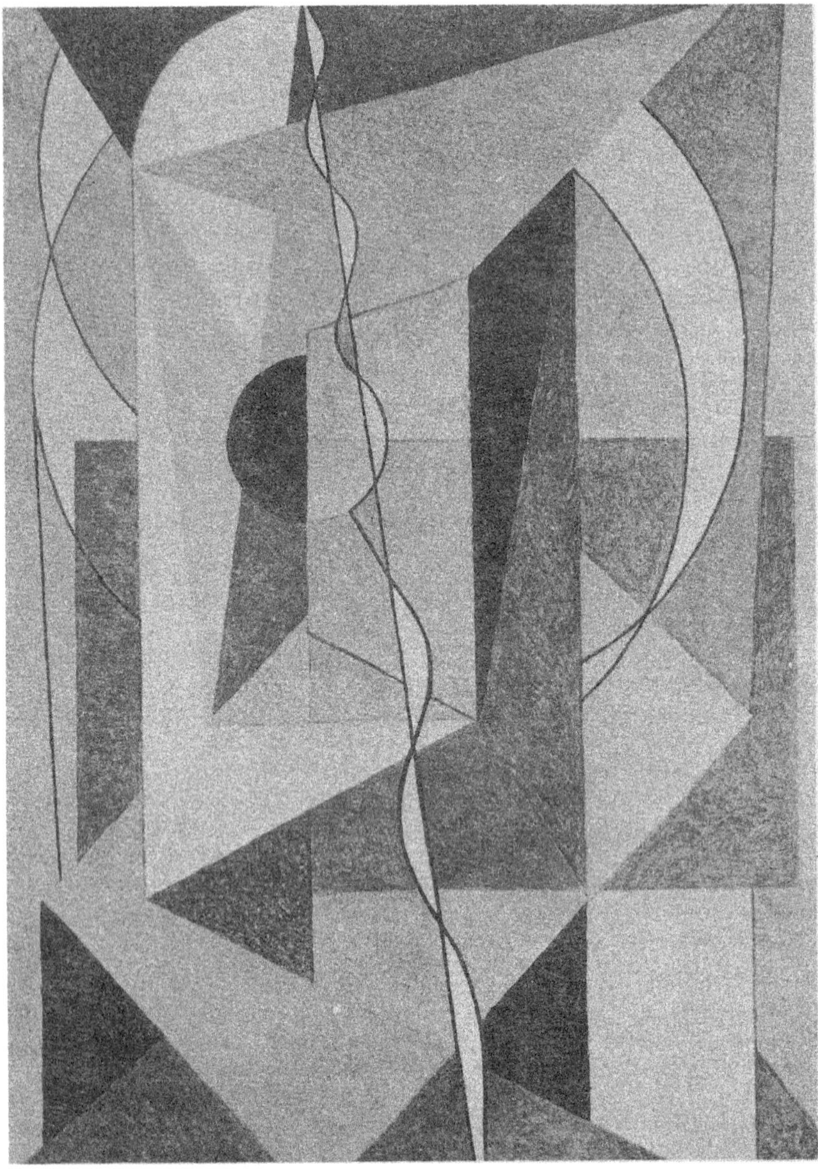

The all-important sphere in the left upper middle section symbolizes, among other things, the sun. Sun worship was "the oldest and by far the most prevalent of all the ancient religions."[15] The sphere is bisected and quartered. "The phenomena of nature that made the deepest religious impression on archaic man [were] the outstretched heavens above him, and the outspread earth beneath; both of which he naturally divided into four quarters . . . this four-fold heaven and earth he signified by a circle, or a square, divided cross-ways."[16] The circle is met within every form of sorcery. The circle in quadrants is called the Magic Circle.[17]

The objects in the Meditation Room are intended to be evocative, in the religious sense. Of what? The mural and altar are admittedly symbols. "By symbolism the simplest, the commonest objects are transformed, idealized, and acquire a new and, so to say, an illimitable value."[18]

An expert[19] on these subjects has written: "Under occult dominion Art, Music and Politics all tend to the same end: confusion, a calculated and inducted confusion: for minds that are confused will *obey* and *bow to* the hidden masters!

"The rule of the Triangle and the Ellipse, together with a crude Geometry in modern art, is the rule . . . in aesthetics.

"Standing before a meaningless Cubist canvas at an art exhibition one day, a puzzled amateur asked 'But what does it mean?' To which the painter replied, 'It's not a question of what it means, it's a question of what is its effect on the observer.'

"Consciously or unconsciously the artist spoke the truth. Psychiatrists tell us that this school of insidious humbug is simply an elaboration of the policy of *the interruption of ideas* leading to total incoherence and madness. 'Cubist' art is an effort to produce certain psychic effects obtainable by optical illusion. Beauty has nothing to do with it. The cubist school is not the realm of art at all. It belongs to that of medicine and psychic science. Those who forget that this devastating fad of 'The Interrupted Idea' can be extended to music, literature and every other phase of human effort, do so at their own peril.

"A mind that is positive cannot be controlled. For the purposes of occult dominion minds must therefore be rendered passive and negative in order that control can be achieved. Minds consciously working to a definite end are a power, and power can oppose power for good or for evil. The scheme for world dominion might be doomed by the recognition of this principle alone, but, as it is unfortunately unrecognized, it remains unchallenged."

THE TETRAGRAMMATON

A striking feature of the mural is the white half-crescent in its upper right quadrant. The inner curve of the crescent — closest to the bisected black, pale-blue and yellow sphere — is equidistant at all points from the exact center of the bisected figure. Therefore, if the curve of the crescent is continued full-circle, the figure which results is a hidden point within a circle, the symbol which was adopted by the astronomers as their sign of the sun. In the Ancient

Mysteries the point in the circle denoted the principle of fecundity and has been carried down through the ages as a sign of various secret societies, including the Illuminati of Adam Weishaupt in 1776.[20] The female principle is also emphasized by the crescent moon or lunette figure.

There are 72 geometrical figures (and shadings) in the mural. The two crescent shapes and the four long triangles — white, yellow, blue and black — which are located in the two upper tiers of the mural, are each counted as one figure. The number 72 denoted from the earliest days the Divine Name of 72 words. This number is derived from a permutation of the values assigned to the four letters of the Tetragrammaton (JHVH: Jehovah), the Ineffable, Unpronounceable Name of God. This Name, in its multitude of forms, can be used to work miracles or magic, so say the Cabalists. It was derived from Exodus xiv, verses 19, 20 and 21, which each consist of 72 letters. "Now, if these three verses be written at length one above another, the first from right to left, the second from left to right, and the third from right to left (or, as the Greeks would say, *boustrophedon*), they will give 72 columns of three letters each. Then each column will be a word of three letters, and as there are 72 columns, there will be 72 words of three letters, each of which will be the 72 names of the Deity alluded to in the text. And these are called the Shemhamforesh." Seventy-two is also the number of the Quinaries or sets of five degrees in the 360 degrees of the Zodiac.[21]

The number of triangles in the mural are difficult to count. There are 22 — isosceles, equilateral, scalene, right-angled — triangles. There are also 22 numbered letters in the ancient Hebrew alphabet, with values of 1 to 400. The triangle is an ancient emblem of Deity; it is also a sign of the female element. However, if the apex of the triangle is pointed down it becomes the male element; thus inverted it may also represent Lucifer, particularly if it is black in color.

The spiral figure intertwined with the mural-length diagonal line symbolizes the Caduceus of Hermes (Mercury), which mythologically is represented as two serpents twined around the winged wand of Mercury. Nine arcs are formed by the intersections of the spiral line with the diagonal; the ninth Hebrew letter, Teth, with the value of nine, has the signification of "serpent."[22] The number of the Beast of Revelation is 666, which cabalistically is nine, the number of generation.[23] The twin serpents of the caduceus are negative and positive (representing polarity) and twine around the spinal column. They are the Kundalini or Sex Force. In *The Encircled Serpent* (Howey, *op. cit.*), the chapter on the Caduceus contains references (page 72) to the ancient use of the symbol without wings, as seen in the mural. The caduceus is also the symbol of peace, the propaganda term associated with the U.N. The serpents are male and female; the sun-god and the moon-god; and are symbols of generation. Buddha was symbolized by the serpent and in mythology is identical with Mercury.

The center sphere and the outer circles around it form the ALL-SEEING EYE. This bisected sphere overlays an isoceles triangle bounded on one side by the diagonal line. According to Manly Palmer Hall, in his occult treatise on *The Secret Destiny of America*,[24] the ALL-SEEING EYE is that of the Great Architect of the Universe (whenever it appears as a symbol of God). His explanation is that which is generally accepted. It is, however, erroneous. A full commentary on the meaning of this all-important symbol appears in Part II of this study.

THE SEPHIROTH

Earlier, reference was made to the Sephiroth, and to the Three Pillars of which it is composed in the form called the Tree of Life. The verses of Exodus which contain the 72 letters of the Tetragrammaton are also believed by the Cabalists to contain the pillars of the Sephiroth, or Emanations. (*The Cabala*, by Bernhard Pick, Chicago, 1913, p. 91.)

The reader will notice in the upper left corner of the mural an arc which curves down to the left from the tip end of the caduceus line and forms the third side of a white geometrical figure which is unique in the mural. The lower end of this arc meets the apex of four triangles — two white, one gray, and one yellow, the last of which touches the perimeter of the black and blue sphere. This arc represents the Crown of the Sephiroth, the first of the ten emanations issued from En Soph, The Divine Darkness (Waite, *op. cit.*, p. 26). The four triangles represent other emanations. The caduceus line symbolizes the spinal chord of Adam Kadmon, The Archetypal Man, another form of the Sephiroth (Pick, *op. cit.*, p. 70). The quartered sphere represents the four different worlds of the Tree. The three rows up and down of the mural are the Three Pillars of the Tree. The 22 triangles in the mural are the 22 lines or paths by which the ten Sephiroth are connected one to another (Waite, *op. cit.*, p. 38). The left, male side of the Tree, indicated by the black half of the sphere, is darkness and death (*Ibid.*, p. 350). The right side of the Tree is female: as symbolized by the moon figure, the white half-crescent. The caduceus line — spinal chord is the sex force which extends down the middle pillar of the Sephiroth, which is also the body of Adam Kadmon. The base of the spine is the Yesod or Foundation, the Sacred generative organs (*Ibid.*, p. 120). From Yesod springs the Kingdom at the bottom of the Tree, which represents Mankind.

The literature on this subject is vast and confusing, but there are certain basic ideas to be found in all cabalistic writings. Bernhard Pick (*op. cit.*, p. 104-5) has written that "the idea of God according to the writings of the Old and new Testaments is entirely different. The same is the case with the notion of creation . . . the Cabala teaches not the Trinity, but the Ten-Trinity of God." Furthermore, man has power over God, for "when the Cabalist prays, God shakes his head, changes at once his decrees, and abolishes heavy judgments." (*Ibid.*, p. 97.)

THE SECRET OF THE ROOM

The mural was described as having been designed to give a feeling of space by the opening up of the wall. All right, let us be literal about this and open up the wall behind the mural. The Meditation Room is constructed in the shape of a wedge. If the reader in his mind's eye looks at the room *from above,* in terms of its shape as a plane figure he will see at once that it is a triangle (pyramid) with the apex (capstone) cut off. (See Part II of this study.) If the two converging lines of the sides of the triangle are extended past the sides of the mural into the empty space beyond the wall, they meet to form the apex of the triangle (capstone of the pyramid). And what have we learned is the overall meaning of the mural? It is that it represents the Tetragrammaton which is symbolized by the Eye in the Triangle. Thus we see that the Meditation Room symbolically represents a full triangle (pyramid) with an invisible apex (capstone) which contains the ALL-SEEING EYE of the mural.

CONCLUSION

The ultramundane symbolism and atmosphere of the Meditation Room of the United Nations may bemuse the unwary and the lukewarm in faith; their delusion need not be shared by Christians or members of other faiths who do not accept ancient paganism clothed in modern dress. "Pagan" had at one time an antonym: *milites Christi* or "enrolled soldiers of Christ"—men and women who fought paganism with every iota of strength and faith and knowledge at their command. *Milites Christi* are needed now to combat the influence and supporters of this Temple of Abomination, with its crude, occult-evoking simulacra of Deity.

St. Paul said (Acts 17, verse 29): "If therefore we are the offspring of God, we ought not to imagine that the Divinity is like to gold or silver or stone, to an image graven by human art and thought." But Hammarskjold likened the light over the altar to the Sun's illumination and the altar to "the God whom man worships under many names and in many forms." Beelzebub or Buddha, Confucius or Christ — they are all one in the Meditation Room, a nameless god.

Appendix: MURAL A GIFT OF MARSHALL FIELD FAMILY

Early accounts of the gift of the mural (its cost in terms of labor, etc.) stated that an "anonymous donor" had supplied it to the room. However, the leaflet handed to visitors of the room states that "the fresco is a gift of the Marshall Field family, in his memory."

Marshall Field was the publisher of the newspaper *PM* in New York City, "sometimes referred to as the uptown edition of the *Daily Worker*";[25] an honorary vice chairman, with Owen Lattimore, of the American Committee in Aid of Chinese Industrial Cooperatives (INDUSCO, Inc.) in 1950, cited as "an organization that is now serving Communist purposes" by the Senate Internal Security Subcommittee;[26] a sponsor of the American Committee for Yugoslav Relief in 1945, declared "subversive and Communist by Attorney General Tom C. Clark";[27] sponsor of a Testimonial Dinner for Fredinand C. Smith in 1944, a cited Communist-front enterprise;[28] and President of the Field Foundation, investigated by the Select Committee To Investigate Tax-Exempt Foundations in 1952 because of its contributions to Communist-front organizations. The Field Foundation's one-time secretary,

Louis S. Weiss, now deceased, was identified in the Committee's hearings as "a member of the Communist Party" (see *American Mercury*, January 1960, page 9). Trustees of the Foundation, namely Channing Tobias and Justine Wise Polier, were cited as long-time Communist-fronters.[29]

SOURCES

1. *New Yorker*, December 28, 1957.
2. "Van Nostrand's Scientific Encyclopedia," 3rd Edition, 1958, p. 1013.
3. November 11, 1957.
4. "In Search of The Miraculous," Harcourt Brace and Co., pp. 26-27.
5. *New York Times* release, December 6, 1950.
6. *UN Room*, Laymen's Movement for a Christian World.
7. UN release, November 1955.
8. *UN Review*, June 1957.
9. "An Encyclopedia of Freemasonry," Albert G. Mackey, New York, 1900, p. 186.
10. Ibid., pp. 750-757.
11. Ibid., pp. 756-757.
12. Ibid., p. 60.
13. Ibid., p. 535.
14. Ibid., p. 481.
15. Ibid., p. 766.
16. "The Migration of Symbols," by Count Goblet d'Alviella, University Books, 1956, p. xiv.
17. "A Pictorial Anthology of Witchcraft, Magic and Alchemy," by Emile Grillot De Givry, University Books, New York, American Edition, 1958, figure 77, page 106.
18. Alviella, op. cit., pp. 1-2.
19. "Occult Theocrasy," by Lady Queenborough (Edith Starr Miller), printed in France, 1933, Volume II, pp. 580-581.
20. A. Mackey, op. cit., p. 590.
21. "The Kabbalah Unveiled," by S. L. M. Mathers, 6th Edition, 1951, Kegan Paul, London, p. 170.
22. S. Mathers, op. cit., p. 3.
23. "Lightbearers of Darkness," by Inquire Within, Boswell Co., London, 1930, p. 106.
24. Philosophical Research Society, Los Angeles, 1950.
25. House Un-American Activities Committee, Rept. 2277, 1942, p. 3.
26. Senate Internal Security Subcommittee, Institute of Pacific Relations hearings, 1952, p. 3793.
27. HUAC Rept. on American Slav Congress, 1950, pp. 81, 122.
28. HUAC Appendix IX, 1944, p. 1623.
29. Hearings, pp. 436 et seq., 726.

MDCCLXXVI

PART II

The Great Seal of the United States

THE GREAT SEAL ON THE DOLLAR BILL

The strange and fascinating history of the Great Seal of the United States has been included in this study because, One, the symbolism of the Meditation Room mural centers around the All-Seeing Eye which also appears above the pyramid on the reverse side of the Great Seal; Two, both sides of the Seal are prominent features of the mosaic window in the Prayer Room in the United States Capitol; Three, the All-Seeing Eye is symbolized in the Temple of Understanding; and Four, both sides of the Seal appear on the one dollar bill because of the same occult influence as was involved in the establishment of the Meditation Room, Prayer Room and the Temple of Understanding.

Arthur M. Schlesinger Jr., in his book, *The Coming of the New Deal,* published in 1958, provided his readers with a remarkably candid portrait of Henry A. Wallace, one-time Vice President of the United States. According to Schlesinger (pp. 31-33):

> The occult fascinated him. He saw special significance in the Great Seal of the United States, with its phrase *E Pluribus Unum* and its conception of unity out of diversity; even more in the reverse of the Seal – the incomplete pyramid, with its thirteen levels of stone and the apex suspended above in the form of an all-seeing eye, surrounded by the inscription *Annuit Coeptis* [and] *Novus Ordo Seclorum....*
>
> Those who are devout believers in the prophecies of the Bible... might well wonder whether the reverse of the Great Seal did not prefigure the Second Coming of the Messiah. Though he remained noncommittal about the extent of his own belief, Wallace did induce the Secretary of the Treasury to put the Great Pyramid on the new dollar bill in 1935. He sold this to Secretary Morgenthau on the prosaic ground that *Novus Ordo* was Latin for New Deal, and for years afterward Morgenthau was beset by people who assumed that the appearance of the Great Pyramid on the currency signified his own attachment to some esoteric fellowship.
>
> His susceptibility to the occult had drawn Wallace in the late twenties into the orbit of a White Russian mystic in the tradition of Blavatsky named Dr. Nicholas Roerich, a painter and an associate in the Moscow Art Theater and the Diaghilev Ballet, a friend of Stravinsky and of Rabindranath Tagore.... Wallace occasionally called on him at the Roerich Museum on Riverside Drive in New York. The friendship continued after Wallace went to Washington... he found solace in a strange and protracted correspondence with Roerich and certain of his disciples. The letters, some addressing Roerich as 'Dear Guru,' contained cabalistic references to 'the Flaming One' or 'the Wavering One' or 'the Mediocre One,' by which he seems to have

meant Roosevelt, 'the Sour One' (Cordell Hull), 'the Dark Ones' or 'the Tigers' (the Soviet Union), and mystic allusions to the chalice with the flame above it and to the descent of America into the depths of purifying fires.

Henry Wallace's deep interest in Roerich's own symbol, three circles in a sphere, was indicated in his book, *New Frontiers*, New York, pp. 11, 17, and 269; and his correspondence with his Dear Guru was reported on at length by Westbrook Pegler in March and April 1948. Wallace's decades-long association with Communists and even espionage agents (like Owen Lattimore) culminated in his candidacy for the Progressive Party, which was nothing more nor less than the Communist Party under a false label.

According to the original Press Release of the Treasury Department (No-5-59, August 15, 1935) announcing the appearance of the two sides of the Seal on the dollar bill, the Latin mottos on the reverse side are translated as "He (God) favored our undertakings" *(Annuit Coeptis)* and "A New Order of the Ages" *(Novus Ordo Seclorum)*. "The eye and triangular glory symbolize an all-seeing Deity. The pyramid is the symbol of strength and its unfinished condition denoted the belief of the designers of the Great Seal that there was still work to be done."

THE EARLY HISTORY OF THE GREAT SEAL

The finest source of information for those who are interested in the early history of the Seal is a thick two-volume study written by C. A. L. Totten in 1882.[1] He is the only authority cited by Gaillard Hunt, author of the State Department's pamphlet, *The History of the Seal of the United States*, published in 1909.

Thomas Jefferson, John Adams and Benjamin Franklin (as chairman) were appointed as a committee by the Continental Congress on July 4, 1776 to prepare a seal for the "United States of America," which meant the 13 states united in the act of independence, and *not* the central government of today (Journals of Congress, 1776, Vol. 1, pp. 248, 397). Jefferson secured the services of a French West Indian portrait painter named Eugene Pierre Du Simitiere, who later did the head of George Washington which was used on the 1791 coin.[2] The All-Seeing Eye appeared on Du Simitiere's first sketch of the seal, as the Eye of Providence—"an adoption of a very ancient symbol of the Overseeing God." Franklin's own choice for a design was an old illustration of Moses crossing the Red Sea accompanied by a quotation attributed to Oliver Cromwell, "Rebellion To Tyrants Is Obedience To God."[3] Nothing came of these first designs; the matter rested until 1782 when Ben Franklin secured William Barton, A.M., a private citizen of Philadelphia, as the second designer. Gaillard Hunt identified William Barton as the son of Reverend Thomas Barton, rector of St. James Episcopal Church, his mother being a sister of the famous David Rittenhouse.[4] William Barton published a memoir of Rittenhouse in 1813.

The first device submitted by Barton depicted among other emblems an Eagle on the summit of a Doric column, the All-Seeing Eye, and the stars:[5]

> The Eagle displayed is the symbol of Supreme Power and Authority, and signifies the Congress; the Pillar, upon which it rests, is used as the Hieroglyphic of Fortitude and Constancy, and, its being of the Doric Order, (which is the best proportioned and most agreeable to Nature,) & Composed of Several Members or parts, all, taken together, forming a beautiful composition of Strength, Congruity and Usefulness, it may with great propriety signify a well planned Government.
>
> * * * [The] stars upon a blue Canton, disposed in a Circle, represent a new Constellation, which alludes to the New Empire, formed in the World by the Confederation of those States. * * * Their disposition, in the form of a Circle, denotes the Perpetuity of its Continuance, the Ring being the Symbol of Eternity.

William Barton's second device transferred the All-Seeing Eye to the reverse side of the Seal; pushed the Eagle up to the Crest; and placed a phoenix rising from the flames at the summit of the column.[6] "The Phoenix is emblematical of the expiring liberty of Britain, revived by her Descendants in America." The second device was adopted, reported on May 9, 1782 and referred to the Secretary of Congress, Charles Thomson, on June 13th. The final device, however, was a composite result of the ideas of Barton, Thomson and Jefferson, who, for example, is known to have placed a triangle around the eye, and to have added the year 1776, *E Pluribus Unum,* and other items.[7] Charles Thomson added the olive branch to the obverse side, and placed the stars above the Eagle as the Crest.

The phrase *Annuit Coeptis* was drawn from Virgil: "*Audacibus annue coeptis,*" rendered as "Favor my daring undertaking" (*Aeneid,* Book 9 verse 625; also in *Georgics,* I, 40). *Novus Ordo Seclorum* was taken from Virgil's 4th Eclogue, 5th Verse: "*Magnus ab integro seclorum nascitur ordo,*" translated "The great series of ages begins anew." The final device was decided upon on June 20, 1782, by the Continental Congress (and its use continued by the new Federal Government on September 15, 1789). In a few weeks a brass die of the face of the Great Seal — the Coat of Arms of the U.S.A. — was completed and put into use. The reverse side of the Seal was not cut in 1782, nor since. (See, however, footnote * on page 37.)

Although it is a cardinal rule of blazonry that a seal's emblems must never vary, the second engraving of the Seal, prepared in 1841 when the old one became worn out, did vary. It was made by Edward Stabler of Sandy Spring, Maryland and was designed by the French artist R. P. Lamplier Jr.[8] It was known as the Websterian Great Seal, after Daniel Webster, the Secretary of State who ordered it made. It was used until 1885 even though it had 6 arrows rather than 13, less than 13 olives on the branch, 6 broadened pales on the escutcheon (shield), and other defects. Totten described it as "a manifest monstrosity" and "illegal and an abortion"— strong terms indeed![9] The third engraving of the Seal was prepared in 1885 under Secretary of State F. T. Frelinghuysen, and the fourth under Secretary John Hay after $1,250 was appropriated on July 1, 1902 for the purpose. The fourth and last die was engraved by Max Zeiler of Philadelphia and cut by Messrs. Bailey, Banks and

Biddle of the same city.[10] Neither of the last two dies were "illegal"— since both conformed in almost all respects to the specifications of the 1782 law. The reproduction of the face of the Great Seal accompanying this study was made from a painting of our heraldic coat of arms, or blazon of the fourth die, which is still in use. The copy of the reverse side was also made from a blazon, not from a die, however, since none was ever made. Both blazons appear as color plates in Gaillard Hunt's *History of the Seal of the United States.*

WHY THE REVERSE SEAL HAS NEVER BEEN USED

As a direct result of prolonged agitation by C. A. L. Totten the U. S. Congress appropriated $1,000 on July 7, 1884 "to obtain dies of the obverse and reverse" sides of the Great Seal (23 Statutes, 354). Totten had objected so strongly to the use of the illegal Websterian Seal that Secretary of State Frelinghuysen had a committee formed under Theodore F. Dwight, chief of the Bureau of Rolls and Library of the State Department, to consider what steps should be taken to revise the design. The committee consultants were Justin Winsor, a history scholar; Professor Charles Eliot Norton of Harvard University; William H. Whitmore, geneologist and author of *Elements of Heraldry* (N. Y. 1866); John Denison Chaplin Jr., Associate Editor of *American Cyclopedia;* and James Horton Whitehouse, designer for Tiffany and Company in New York City.[11]

The five men recommended that the reverse side of the Seal not be cut and not be used as an official document seal. Professor Norton wrote that "it is greatly to be regretted that the device adopted by Congress in 1782 is of so elaborate and allegorical a character. As to the reverse . . . it can hardly (however artistically treated by the designer) look otherwise than as a dull emblem of a Masonic fraternity."[12] Justin Winsor described the reverse side as "both unintelligent and commonplace. If it can be kept in the dark, as it seems to have been kept, why not keep it so?" T. F. Dwight also felt that "it has been so long kept in the dark, a few months more of shade will do it no harm." William Whitmore considered it "a thankless task to arrange it, as Professor Norton says; use it as little as possible." J. D. Chaplin Jr. objected to the Crest of stars on the obverse side: "This is bad, very bad, heraldically." He also noted that "the law does not call for 13 courses of stone" in the pyramid on the reverse side.[13] "So general was the criticism of it (the reverse) and so palpable were its shortcomings that it was determined not to cut it."[14] During the 1892 World's Fair in Chicago copies of the two sides of the Seal were made for exhibition. However, the appearance presented by the reverse "was so spiritless, prosaic, heavy, and unappropriate that it was never hung."[15]

MYSTIC SYMBOLISM OF REVERSE SEAL

C. A. L. Totten, as a 1st Lieutenant in the 4th Artillery, U. S. Army, communicated his views on thé Seal to Charles J. Folger, Secretary of the Treasury, on February 10, 1882. His plea for the issuance of a medal commemorating the centenary of the adoption of the Seal was successful. He wrote that "the All-Seeing Eye is one of the oldest hieroglyphics of the Deity. The triangle also is a cabalistic symbol of the most remote antiquity. . . .

"The descent of the mystic eye and triangle in the form of a capstone to this mysterious monument [the Great Pyramid of Gizeh] of all times and nations, is to us as a people most pregnant with significance. The motto, *Novus Ordo Seclorum,* is a quotation from the 4th Eclogue and was borrowed in turn by Virgil from the mystic Sybylline records.

"The entire quotation is as follows: 'The last age of Cumaen song now comes. *(Novus Ordo Seclorum* altered from *Magnus Soeclorum ordo),* A mighty order of ages is born anew. Both the prophetic Virgin and Saturnian kingdoms now return. Now a new progeny is let down from the lofty heavens. Favor, chaste Lucina, the boy soon to be born in whom the iron age shall come to an end, and the golden one shall arise again in the whole earth'." Virgil was a pagan philosopher of Rome.[16]

The literature on the mystic meaning of the Seal is extensive and amazing. It appears that almost every secret fraternity, society and movement in the country has claimed the Seal's reverse side as its own. Celestia Root Lang wrote:[17] "The reverse side must have been designed by a mystic, one versed in symbolism. . . . All *true* Theosophists ought to be able to see . . . the connecting link between *true* Theosophy and the *reverse* side of the Seal of the United States. . . . the time will come . . . when the white stone will become the headstone of the corner of our government . . . in proclaiming a *new* religion in which all spiritual currents flowing from every religion shall meet in the perfection of the white stone [capstone over the pyramid] teaching of . . . spiritual unfoldment . . . having neither dogma nor doctrine. . . . We see in Mr. [William] Barton only the facade of the instrument; that, if he himself was not a Mystic or Seer, then, a Master stood behind him." (Her emphasis.) Miss Lang felt that this "Master" must have been Thomas Paine, the Deist and revolutionary.

C. A. L. Totten attributed a Scriptural meaning to the use of the number 13 in the Seal: 13 stripes in the Shield, 13 stars in the Crest, 13 letters in *E Pluribus Unum,* 13 arrows, 13 olive branch leaves, 13 olive berries; and, on the reverse side, 13 courses of stones in the pyramid and 13 letters in *Annuit Coeptis.*[18] He noted that the number 13 occurs twice in one of the forms of the Tetragrammaton: Jehovah: JHVH: J(10) H(5) V(6) H(5): 26: 2 x 13.[19] Another source[20] claimed that the Seal is a symbol of the Rosicrucians and that the clouds represent the "white roses" of the Order. The Federation of British Israelites adopted the reverse side as its own emblem.[21] One of the dies of the face of the Seal shows the dexter wing of the Eagle with 32 feathers and the sinister (left) wing with 33 feathers, which supposedly establishes its connection with the Scottish Rite order.[22] None of these claims are substantiated by any evidence which can be considered conclusive.

THE CREST: THE SEAL OF SOLOMON

The controversy which has swirled around the symbolism of the Great Seal for over 180 years has by no means been limited to the reverse side. The Crest heraldically is an independent device; it is correctly considered apart from the Eagle and from the reverse side of the Seal. As an emblem of Arms selected for special dignity the Crest represents America herself. The Eagle represents the People.

The Crest is composed of the stars, around which is disposed a circle of clouds, and the Glory, a halo or corona of light. Totten wrote that: "The Glory has not been correctly realized upon a single die used for Great Seal purposes. . . . the primary significance of a Glory was to denote the presence of God." Heraldry borrowed this emblem directly from the Scriptures (Ps. lxiii, 2; 1 Kings viii, 11, etc.). Yet, as Totten pointed out, not a single ray of light breaks through the clouds. God thus becomes a captive within the circle (which can represent the Serpent), as Jehovah is a captive of the Cabalists (see Sephiroth, Part 1). Totten discovered that the State Department had dropped the Glory altogether in its representation of the Coat of Arms as an architectural ornament in full color above the entrances of its foreign embassies, legations and consulates throughout the world. The Crest was thus mutilated and the Presence of God was no longer symbolized in the emblem. Tottens comments also apply to the fourth die which is still in use.[23]

The Constellation of Stars — by its arrangement — constitutes the most serious deviation from the Fundamental Law which authorized the establishment of the Seal. The Honorary A. Loudon Snowden, Superintendent of the Mint of the United States, objected to the appearance of the "13 stars embraced in an oblong or depressed circle [which design he considered] doubtless the result of an unappreciative engraver, who imagined the stars would look more artistically arranged if embraced within the lines of a circle." He also objected to the pyramid on the back side because "each layer representing a State, is subdivided, or broken, and as if composed of several pieces cemented together. This was certainly not the original design [for the] unfinished national pyramid."[24] The 13 levels should have been composed of 13 *solid* blocks. Snowden was correct in his objections but naive in his interpretation of the motives of the designer.

In our national heraldry *all* stars are five-pointed. Yet the 13 stars in the Crest are arranged in the form of a six-pointed star which is composed of two interlaced triangles. This is unmistakably the ancient Oriental talisman, the Seal of Solomon. Totten wrote:[25]

> * * * the legal specifications of the group of stars as "a constellation" warrants some degree of regularity in the "heraldic" arrangement * * * But why *now* a *six*-pointed constellation of *five*-pointed stars? This is a clear lapse from the developed standpoint. In the first realization of the Seal, as cut from the original die, the stars were conceived as six-pointed and the constellation was very naturally made six-pointed to match. But the lapse was soon discovered from comparison with the stars upon the Flag, so while they were changed to the five-pointed order in the Websterian die, the six-pointed form of the constellation was unfortunately retained and still mars the realization

of our Crest. It should be manifest that the very same deference paid to an heraldic art-idea, which resulted in grouping thirteen *six*-pointed stars into a larger *six*-pointed constellation, would have grouped them, as *five*-pointed elements, into a corresponding *five*-pointed constellation. [His emphasis.]

Mr. Totten erred in one respect: the incorrectness of the use of six-pointed stars in the Crest was not "soon discovered"—since we know that the Websterian die was not cut until almost *sixty* years later! The "unartistic, unnatural and cramped arrangement" of the stars in the Crest did not occur by mere chance. Mr. Albert C. Hopkins stated flatly that "the arrangement of the stars of the Crest into the form of a six-pointed feudal star is wholly unknown to our Flag whose new Constellation it purports to represent."[26] After the third die was cut in 1885 Totten commented that "the incongruous if not still ominous six-pointed constellation continues to over shadow the Eagle, and its talons are so enormously out of proportion that they look as if they belonged to the well-known monstrous bird of Arabian mythology, the Roc."[27]

A curious fact concerning the original Great Seal seems to have eluded the notice of all the writers who have concerned themselves with its history and significance. The face of the Seal contains the number 13 repeated 6 times (as Totten noted). 13 x 6 equals 78. The 13 six-pointed stars on the original die also repeated this figure (13 x 6: 78), thus establishing an exact numerical balance between the Crest and the entire Coat of Arms.

THE ARMS AND CREST IN ST. PAUL'S CHAPEL, N. Y.

C. A. L. Totten was the first historian to photograph and publicize the painting of the Arms and Crest in St. Paul's Chapel in New York City:[28]

> Immediately after the inauguration of George Washington, their first Constitutional President, Congress adjourned, and in a body proceeded to St. Paul's Chapel, where it engaged in divine service. Upon reorganizing, it ordered that a duly blazoned, and framed painting of the Arms of the Crest of the United States should be prepared, and suspended over the President's pew in St. Paul's. This painting hangs today in its appropriate place. . . . it is . . . of immense value as a link in the history of our national heraldry. It speaks with the highest authority upon some of the disputed points. . . .
>
> It is the first and only blazon of its kind ever ordered by Congress. . . . One of the most interesting features of this celebrated blazon is the fact that its artist — (name unknown) — conceived aright the natural arrangement of the Crest or Constellation. The stars in this blazonry, which by the way are correctly *five-pointed*, are arranged *irregularly* over the field, and not circumscribed or confined in a circle . . . . the clouds which surround the group . . . roll back and break away in a marked circular form. Thus the emblem of eternity — the circle — . . . does not in any way limit the group. Its very arrangement implies the future growth of the new constellation, as rolling further back the clouds shall let in other stars until a form results whose stellar distribu-

tion we cannot even dimly yet discern. . . . The marked avoidence, too, of their arrangement in the form of a six-pointed constellation of six-pointed stars is also noticeable. [His emphasis.]

The original painting of the Arms and Crest, executed after Washington's inauguration on April 30, 1789, still hangs in its appointed place over the President's pew in the North Aisle of St. Paul's Chapel at Broadway and Fulton Street, New York City, where it may be seen by visitors any day of the week. A 5¢ picture postcard of the painting is sold in the Chapel.

St. Paul's Chapel is the oldest public building on Manhattan Island, erected in 1766. Here George Washington worshipped for two years (see *Washington's Diary*, 1789 and 1790), seated directly under the beautiful and inspiring painting of our national Coat of Arms hanging on the wall behind his pew. The religious heritage of our Nation could hardly have been expressed in a more felicitous fashion than it was in the symbolism of this painting. The Glory of golden light is by far the most prominent feature of the blazon. It indicates in the strongest terms the Presence of God. The heavenly rays of light extend from the outer perimeter of the circle of clouds out behind the entire upper portion of the Eagle's body and even beyond the tips of its wings. The head of the Eagle with its fierce curved beak is *within* the circle of clouds. No occult meaning can be attached to the number of feathers in the wings and tail. The escutcheon (shield) on the breast is curved; its sides meet in a point at the base of the tail. The curved shield is heraldically correct and has far greater esthetic appeal than the square shield on the official Coat of Arms.

On the wall beneath the painting is a brass plaque bearing the text of George Washington's Prayer for the United States of America:

Almighty God; we make our earnest prayer that Thou wilt keep the United States in Thy holy protection, that Thou wilt incline the hearts of the citizens to cultivate a spirit of subordination and obedience to government; and entertain a brotherly affection and love for one another and for their fellow citizens of the United States at large. And finally that Thou wilt most graciously be pleased to dispose us all to do justice, to love mercy and to demean ourselves with that charity, humility and pacific temper of mind which were the characteristics of *the Divine Author of our blessed religion,* and without a humble imitation of whose example in these things we can never hope to be a happy nation. Grant our supplication, we beseech Thee, *through Jesus Christ Our Lord.* Amen. [Emphasis supplied.]

Washington's Prayer was adapted from his Circular Letter to the Governors; its use of the phrase, "our blessed religion," reflected in unmistakable terms Washington's conviction that the United States was a Christian Nation.

A very early drawing in *Columbian Magazine*[29] of the Coat of Arms shows the constellation of *five*-pointed stars scattered over the whole field, as in the painting in St. Paul's Chapel. It's Glory also breaks through the clouds. However, the stars on the Washington Medal (1792) made at the Mint by Dr. Rittenhouse were six-pointed and its olive branch leaves were 15 rather than 13 in number.[30] The Diplomatic Medal also showed the Glory "breaking through the clouds"[31] and the Great Seal Centenary Medal of 1882 did not depict the Seal of Solomon on the Crest.[32] *Harper's Weekly* reported during the year the Centenary Medal was struck that "in all that pertains to heraldry it is inaccurate" (referring to both sides of the Seal) and that officials of the Treasury and State Departments were considering scrapping the Great Seal for a new design.[33] Samuel Lewis, a jeweler in Washington, D.C., prepared a 20 pound steel die for a Great Treaty Seal which showed *60* leaves on the olive branch and *six*-pointed stars in the Seal of Solomon Crest. It was used until 1883.[34]

An unknown engraver placed the unfinished pyramid on the $50.00 bill of 1778.[35] The *Nova Constellatio* colonial coins, 1783-85, showed on their obverse sides the Radiant Eye;[36] and the 3 cent silver piece in use from 1851 to 1873 was engraved with the Seal of Solomon.[37] It is also very important to know that Congress ordered the preparation of a smaller seal for the personal use of all the Presidents of the Confederation. *It consisted of one emblem only: the Seal of Solomon Crest.*[38] The Kentucky penny of 1791 was adorned with a triangle of 15 stars.[39] The use of these symbols on the coins, currency and the small seal provides us with conclusive proof of the existence of a directing influence behind the adoption of these occult signs at the time of the founding of Our Nation.

C. A. L. Totten provided drawings in his massive study of the correct form in which the Constellation should have appeared in the Crest, presuming any regularity of design was necessary. (See illustration of the design.[40]) It incorporates the Cross in the Constellation and certainly is more appropriate than the Seal of Solomon. There *is* a Southern Cross in the heavens, but no constellation remotely resembling the two interlaced triangles of the design in use.

The heraldry of American heroism never used the Solomonic seal before 1942. The Constellation in the Crest appeared on the four decorations of the Legion of Merit, created by Congress July 20, 1942. The degrees of Chief Commander, Commander, Officer and Legionnaire are awarded to the personnel of the armed forces of friendly foreign nations, and of the U. S. and the Philippines. This decoration was the first specific award in U. S. history to foreigners, and the first to have different degrees, as in the secret orders. The Commander award has the motto, *Annuit Coeptis,* along with the emblem. The designer of these decorations, Colonel Townsend Heard, also placed the motto, *Novus Ordo Seclorum,* on the obverse side of the Medal for Merit, awarded to civilians of the United States and her allies by act of Congress 7/20/42.[41]

THE ALL-SEEING EYE A SYMBOL OF OSIRIS

We now arrive at the point when we must consider that all-important key symbol, the All-Seeing Eye. Mr. Totten traced the history of the Eye in the triangle back to ancient Chaldea and its appearance as the Solar Eye, the Eye of Jove or Jupiter, of Phoebus or Apollo, the Eye of Baal, and as the Eye of Providence. The Eye of Jove appeared on the front of Jove's temple at Peloponnessus. As the Solar Eye it was the symbol of the Arabian god of. Jethro, the black father-in-law of Moses, and of the Arabic motto, "Allah," or "I am that I am." All ancient temples of Arabia were decorated with the Eye, which had first appeared as the symbol of Osiris, Isis and Horus of Egypt.[42]

The Eye represented the mystic symbol of the so-called Egyptian "trinity," expressed in these words, often inscribed on the statues of Isis: "I am all that has been, that is, or shall be, and none among mortals has hitherto taken off my veil." She was the daughter of Saturn and her name meant *ancient.* She married her brother Osiris, and was pregnant by him even before she had left her mother's womb, according to Plutarch's account. She and her brother-husband comprehended all nature and all the gods of the heathens. She was the Venus of Cyprus, the Minerva of Athens, the Cybele of the Phrygians, the Ceres of Eleusis, the Proserpine of Sicily, the Diana of Crete, the Bellona of the Romans, &c. And she was the Moon and Osiris the Sun.[43] Osiris received the same adoration as Anubis, Bacchus, Dionysius, Jupiter and Pan. In other words, debauched revelries or saturnalias (from Saturn, his father) were held in his honor. "He visited the greater part of the kingdoms of Asia and Europe, where he enlightened the minds of man by introducing among them the worship of the gods, and a reverence for the wisdom of a supreme being."[44]

Totten, tracing the symbolism of the Eye, affirmed that "the word Jehovah, of the Solar circle of Arabia, superseded the Egyptian motto in the radiant triangle, and as the Word soon became too sacred to be spoken or ever written, it was generally symbolized by the All-Seeing Eye of Him whose name it was."[45] He described the "cap of purest crystal" once atop the pyramid of Gizeh (the floating triangle on the reverse Seal) as the "priceless gem of Egypt"—"the terrible crystal." (Job xxxviii, 4-7.) He believed that "when at last *it* shall actually crown the Pyramid of human institutions, then indeed shall all men dwell beneath the shadow of 'The Rock'."[46] (Deut. xxxii, 4; Psalms xci, 1; Isa. xxvi, 4 and xxxii, 2.) Totten insisted that the symbolism had a Scriptural basis. His "cap" on the pyramid is the Biblical cornerstone; his "Rock" is Jehovah in the Old Testament. Yet his own research and documentation on the meaning of the Seal proved the contrary. He was always the optimist, even when he wrote that he could not "but feel . . . the certainty that a Hidden Hand blazoned the heraldry of this Great People."[47]

George Rawlinson's massive three-volume history of *The Seven Great Monarchies of the Ancient Eastern World*[48] provides us with vital and pertinent data concerning the symbols with which we are dealing. The Babylonians of the 7th Century B.C. attached to each god in their pantheon "a special mystic number, which is used as his emblem and may even stand for his name in an inscription." Further, each god had an emblematic sign. "Thus a circle, plain or crossed, designates the Sun-god, San or Shamas; a six-rayed or eight-rayed star the Sun-goddess, Gula or Anunit." The altar was represented by an emblem surmounted by a triangle.[49] The use of the simple circle and the quartered disk as a divine symbol of the sun traced back from the Babylonians to the Chaldeans of the 23rd Century B.C. The gods were the same, San and Gula; the symbols were the same.[50] The two monarchies placed their gods in triads, headed by one god, Ra, "a sort of fount and origin of deity." San was the second member of the second triad, accompanied by his wife.[51] The first triad consisted of Ana (Pluto), the "Lord of darkness or death;" Belus (Jupiter), the son of the Egyptian Osiris and the god whose temple was the original of the tower of Babel;[52] and Hoa (Neptune), strongly connected "with the serpent of Scripture and . . . the tree of life." Hoa's wife was the mother of Belus.[53] The Cabalists lifted their entire Sephirotic tree of life representing Jehovah from the triads of the Chaldean-Babylonian pantheon (see Sephiroth, Part 1).

The Egyptian pantheon was even more ancient, dating from the 27th to the 30th Centuries B.C. or even earlier, according to some sources. The Sun-gods of Egypt were nine in number. The chief among them was Osiris, whose worship was universal. He was "the great deity of Amenti or Hades [Hell]." Rawlinson described Osiris' role as the Judge of the Dead: "It was the universal belief that, immediately after death, the soul descended into the lower world and was conducted to the Hall of Truth, where it was judged in the presence of Osiris and the forty-two demons, the 'Lords of Truth' and judges of the dead."[54] (One of the divine names of the Tetragrammaton consisted of 42 letters.) Osiris was called "the master of the gods." The name of Osiris was expressed, most simply, by two hieroglyphs, one of which was *the human eye* (the left eye, as used on the reverse side of the Great Seal). "Sometimes, however, the human eye is replaced by a simple circle." Osiris was most commonly represented "in a mummied form, to mark his presidency over the dead.... When represented as a man walking, he has the lappeted wig, crowned with two wavy horns, above which are ... two feathers. The wavy horns are also found with the plumed crown above them, and serpents (uraei) on either side, surmounted by disks. . . . Isis, at one time his mother, at another his sister, at another his daughter, is always his wife, and their child is Har or Horus."[55]

The 42 demons who aided Osiris in the infernal regions were known as "the assessors" and had such names as "eyes of flame," "breath of flame," "cracker of bones," "devourer of shades," "eater of hearts," "swallower," "white tooth," and "smoking face." They "lived by catching the wicked," "fed off their blood," and "devoured their hearts before Horus." They were judges, accusers and punishers of crime. "Guilty souls were handed over to them by Osiris, but to be 'tortured' only, not destroyed."[56]

During Osiris' great expedition beyond the borders of Egypt "he left his kingdom to the care of his wife Isis, and her faithful minister Hermes or Mercury" who was Anubis (brother to Osiris), represented with a *caduceus*. When Osiris returned he found that his brother Set (Typhon) had aroused his subjects against him. (Set's name was expressed by a hieroglyphic containing the black half-sphere seen in the meditation room mural.) Set murdered his brother and cut his body *into fourteen pieces*. Isis recovered all the mangled pieces, with the exception of the privities of her husband, which had been thrown into the sea. Horus defeated Set and Osiris was proclaimed to be a resurrected god. His body, encased in fourteen different statues, was worshipped with divine honors. That part of the body not recovered was rendered homage during festivals called *Phallica*, which were introduced into Europe by the Athenians. The entire system of phallic worship in the ancient world originated in this festival held in honor of Osiris.[57]

The number *fourteen* has a special occult meaning in the symbolism of modern-day secret societies as the "14 days of burial (lunar darkness)." Plutarch, in his treatise *On Isis and Osiris*, explained the symbolism: "The body of Osiris was cut into *fourteen* pieces; that is, into as many parts as there are days between the full moon and the new."[58] Now, if the picture of the reverse side of the Great Seal is examined, it will be found that *fourteen* rays of light issue from the triangle containing the Eye of Osiris. This combination of symbols simply cannot be attributed to a chance arrangement.

Only one writer — an occultist — has realized the startling fact that the number of stones in the pyramid totals 72, the 72 arrangements of the Tetragrammaton, the cabalistic name of Jehovah.[59] The stones are counted as follows (from the top 13th level down to the base): 3; 4; 4(3 plus 2 ½'s); 4; 5; 5(4 plus 2 ½'s); 5; 6; 6(5 plus 2 ½'s); 7(6 plus 2 ½'s); 7; 8; 8(7 plus 2 ½'s). Total: 72. The meaning of the Tetragrammaton was explained at length in Part I.

The pagan origin of the two mottos on the reverse seal has already been attested to. The entire quotation cited earlier containing the phrase *Novus Ordo Seclorum* provides the clue as to the nature of the "New Order of the

Ages" referred to. It is a "golden" age during which the "Saturnian" kingdom shall return. Saturn was the father of Osiris. The other motto, *Annuit Coeptis,* "Favor my daring undertaking," was *not* a supplication to God; in conjunction with the other motto it can only refer to Saturn or Osiris. The reign of Saturn was called "the golden age" even though he received human sacrifices and devoured his own children. He was symbolized by the serpent biting its own tail.[60]

THE SUN AND THE SERPENT

Ophiolatry is the worship of serpents. The religion of ancient Egypt was closely interwoven with the worship of sun and serpent. The deity, Kneph, was pictured as a serpent in a fiery circle. "He was regarded as the first emanation of the Supreme Being, the good genius of the world, the demiurgus, the efficient Reason of all things, and the Architect of the Universe. . . . Kneph is identified with the sun, hence the rays of glory around his head. Both pent and sun were emblems of the Celestial Father. . . . As the solar deity, Kneph became the Cristos of the Gnostics. . . . was regarded as the spiritual sun of enlightenment, or wisdom."[61]

In the Egyptian pantheon, "Osiris himself was said to have been the son of Kneph . . . and he was essentially identical with Kneph." The worship of Isis, the moon-goddess, was equally entwined with ophiolatry. Her emblem was the horned viper. "In the British Museum there is a head of Isis wearing a coronet of them." The Egyptians often represented Isis and Osiris together, as two serpents. "About the commencement of the Christian era the cult of Osiris was extended over Asia Minor, Greece and Rome." Cicero tells us that he was known as Ob-el, from whence we derive the *obelisk.*[62]

The identity of Hermes-Mercury-Anubis (brother to Osiris) has already beeen mentioned. His emblem, the *caduceus,* was the talismanic serpent, originally entwined around a Tau cross, which was also a *phallus.* The serpents represented the power of Mercury as a Sun-god. The *caduceus* was identified with Moses' Brazen Serpent. "In Judah the image of Jehovah took the form of a golden serpent, as in Solomon's temple." Its worship "was in fact the worship of the Sun-god, Osiris, under the name of Jehovah." The *Targum,* or *Chaldee Paraphrast,* referred to the Brazen Serpent as the 'Word'."[63] It must also be mentioned that the olive branch on the Coat of Arms — the emblem of peace — traces directly back to the olive wand of the *caduceus.*[64]

The Cao Dai God Symbol: The All-Seeing Eye

Today, in South Viet Nam in South-east Asia there exists a very real Cult of the All-Seeing Eye. It is called Cao Dai. It is a bizarre blend of Buddhism, Confucianism, Taoism, Christianity, and Animism. The last named doctrine refers to the *anima mundi,* the idea that phenomena of animal life are produced by an immaterial soul. Ophiolatry is a component part of the Cao Dai "religion" which is symbolized by the God symbol of the All-Seeing Eye in the Triangle (see illustration). The Eye, neither right nor left, has a thick black eyebrow above it. Sixteen rays emanate from the triangle.

The sect claims a membership of two million or more, mostly in the Mekong Delta region and Tay Ninh province, northeast of Saigon, which it once ruled with a private army. Its Great Temple, located near the Cambodian border in the same area, contains great columns around which are entwined raised carvings of huge cobras, reaching from the floor to the ceiling. The Cao Dai "Pope" sits on a serpent throne in this temple. The two arms of the throne are carved into the shape of two huge cobra heads and necks. Two similar cobra heads form the base; and the undersides of three more cobra heads and necks provide the backrest of the throne. The "Pope's" entire royal robe and his foot coverings also represent the shape and skin of the cobra.

The Cao Dai also has its own "cardinals" in its "Vatican" headquarters in the Great Temple, which is 55 miles northeast of Saigon. The cult has deliberately adopted the use of Catholic terms to mock Catholicism. It has an expanding pantheon that includes Clemenceau, Sun Yat-sen, Victor Hugo and Joan of Arc, and, in nomination pending his death, Sir Winston Churchill. Its Pope, Pham Cong Tac, formerly a Saigon customs clerk, died in exile in Cambodia in 1959 and has not yet been replaced. The cult, formed in Saigon in the 1920's, had managed by 1956 to build up a private army of 15,000 men. Pham Cong Tac, to stay in power, at one time or another, allied his army and 2 million supporters with the Japanese, the French, and the Communist guerillas.

The first Premier-President of South Viet Nam, Catholic Ngo Dinh Diem, crushed the Cao Dai cult in 1955-56, with the assistance of Pham Cong Tac's Military Chief-of-Staff General Nguyen Thanh Phuong. The General disarmed the 400-man "papal guard" and clapped a score of "cardinals" and Pham Cong Tac himself under house arrist. In early March, 1956, the General forced the "Pope" into exile in Pnompenh in Cambodia, by collecting certified letters from 19 "vestal virgins" of Cao Dai who complained that Pham Cong Tac had raped them.

The Cao Dai, at the height of its power in 1955, controlled — with two other sects — one-third of South Viet Nam. The three sects formed an exotic consortium of religious fanatics, feudal warlords, uniformed hoodlums and racket bosses. Their combined armies totaled 40,000 men. One of the sects, the Hoa Hao, is composed of dissident Buddhists founded by the deceased Huynh Phu So, who, so the story goes, converted his psychiatrist when he was sent to a lunatic asylum. The other sect, the Binh Xuyen, is an organization of bandits, in mustard-colored uniforms, who controlled both the brothels of Saigon and the police of the same city under an arrangement with the absentee chief of state, Bao Dai. Their commander, General Le Van Vien, was once a river pirate.

Premier Ngo Dinh Diem crushed the three sects. For eight years South Viet Nam was free of the evil of the Cao Dai. Then, in late 1963, the Premier and his brother, Ngo Dinh Nhu, were assassinated in a CIA-supported murder plot headed by Buddhist traitors in the Vietnamese Government. At once the top surviving Cao Dai leader, exiled General Le Than Tat, returned to Viet Nam from Cambodia to regroup the many factions of the cult into a unified movement.

General Tat returned on November 15, 1963 to the fold of the Cao Dai in a solemn ceremony in the Great Temple decorated with its grotesque dragons and the central symbol of the sect – the All-Seeing Eye radiating "cosmic rays." He knelt before an altar of sculpted cobras and a portrait of Victor Hugo in the uniform of the French Academy. The elaborate ritual performed by the "priests" at that time represented an obscene travesty of religion. The central object of worship is the Serpent. The cult of the All-Seeing Eye, the Cao Dai, openly worships the same ancient deity that its American counterpart venerates and adores behind a screen of mummery and Mumbo Jumbo.[65]

*See page 25.–"The Seal of the United States" (State Dept. Pub. No. 6455, issued 1957, 30¢ per copy, Superintendent of Documents, U.S. Govt. Printing Off., Washington 25, D.C.), lists cuttings of the Seal not previously recorded: an "illegal" Great Treaty Seal die cut in 1825 by Seraphim Masi, jeweler, Washington, D.C.; an "illegal" die of the obverse side of the Seal cut in 1877 by Herman Baumgarten of Washington. It states that the 1841 die was cut by John V. N. Throop of Washington and that the 1885 die was cut by Tiffany and Co. of New York. It also notes that "evidence has recently been found" indicating that in 1885 "a die may then have in fact been cut" of the *reverse side* of the Seal – which was never put in use. The original 1782 die is on display in the National Archives and the other dies may be seen on the north mezzanine of the main State Dept. building. The Custodian of the Great Seal refuses to allow any examination of the files in her possession by historians even though the Seal is uniquely a part of our National Inheritance. It is *the* symbol of America, the People, and the Congress.

SOURCES

1. "Our Inheritance In the Great Seal of the United States and Its Signification unto 'The Great People' Thus Sealed." Vol. I, Its History and Heraldry (Published in March 1897 by the Our Race Pub. Co., Study No. 18, Copyright 1882), by Charles Adiel Lewis Totten; Vol. II, The Seal of History, Signification, Facts of Note (Yale University, Quarterly, *Our Race*—Its Origin and Its Destiny, Series V, No. 19, 1897, New Haven, Conn.).
2. Ibid., I, p. 9; see also *Harper's Mag.* July 1856, Vol. III, p 179, & *Mag. of Amer. History*, June 1893.
3. Ibid., I, p. 41.
4. *Pennsylvania Magazine*, X, p. 414.
5. "The History of the Seal of the United States." by Gaillard Hunt, State Department, Washington. D.C., 1909.
6. Ibid., pp. 28, 30.
7. Totten, op. cit., I. p. 11.
8. Ibid., p. 256.
9. Ibid., I, pp. 210, 212; II, p. 226; see also *Galaxy*, Vol. 23, p. 691, May 1877, "The Great Seal of the United States."
10. Hunt, op. cit., p. 61.
11. Ibid., p. 54.
12. Ibid., p. 55; see also "The Unfinished Work of the USA," by De Vos, "Its Origin, Mission, And Destiny As Revealed in Its Unused Seal & The Holy Scriptures," New Age Pub. Co.. Coopersville, Mich., 1921, p. 87.
13. Hunt, op. cit., pp. 56, 58.
14. De Vos, op. cit., p. 86.
15. Hunt, op. cit., p. 61.
16. Totten, op. cit., I, p. 71.
17. Ed. and Pub. of *Divine Life Mag.* (Independent Theosophical Soc. of Amer.), Chicago, 5/15/17. "The Reverse Side of the Seal of the United States and Its Symbolism," pp. 1, 7, 8, 9.
18. Quoted by Theodore Heline in "America's Destiny — A New Order of The Ages," New Age Press, Los Angeles, 1941. p. 10.
19. Totten, op. cit., II, p. 98.
20. "Mystic Americanism," by Grace Kincaid Morey, Eastern Star Pub. Co., E. Aurora, N. Y., 1924, p. 65.
21. *Modern Mystic*, August 1939, Washington, D. C., p. 307.
22. Ibid., July 1939, p. 250.
23. Totten, op. cit., I, p. 256; II, pp. 179, 194, 201, 203.
24. Correspondence Between Hon. Chas. J. Folger, Sec. of the Treasury, & Hon. A Loudon Snowden, Super. of the U.S. Mint. Relative to Striking a Medal in Commemoration of the Adoption of the Great Seal of the U. S., 2/19/82, 2/21/82 (Pub. 1885): see also *Philadelphia Ledger*, 6/24/82 & Totten, op. cit., I, p. 179.
25. Totten, op. cit., I, p. 140; II, p. 179.
26. Ibid., II, pp. 179, 186.

27. Ibid., I, p. 218.
28. Ibid., pp. 137, 138.
29. Sept. 1786; see also Totten, op. cit., I, p. 13.
30. Totten, op. cit., I, p. 146.
31. Ibid., p. 152.
32. Ibid., II, p. 191.
33. 11/25/82, p. 739.
34. Totten, op. cit., I, p. 161.
35. Hunt, op. cit., p. 41.
36. Totten, op. cit., I, p. 246.
37. Ibid., II, p. 72.
38. Ibid., I, p. 255.
40. Ibid., p. 146.
41. "The Heraldry of Heroism," by Arthur E. Du Bois, *National Geographic Magazine*, 1943, Plate 1 and p. 414.
42. Totten, op. cit., II, pp. 310-312.
43. Lempriere's "Classical Dictionary," E. P. Dutton & Co., 1949, p. 301.
44. Ibid., p. 561.
45. Totten, op. cit., II, p. 312.
46. Ibid., pp. 315, 316.
47. Ibid., p. 253.
48. Also, "The History of Ancient Egypt," in 2 vols. by Geo. Rawlinson, all 5 vols. pub. by The Nottingham Society, 2nd Ed., 1880.
49. Ibid., Vol. II, Medea, Babylonia, Persia, p. 229.
50. Ibid., Vol. I, Chaldea, Assyria, pp. 83, 84.
51. Ibid., pp. 72-74, 79, 82.
52. Lempriere, op. cit., p. 105.
53. Rawlinson, op. cit., I, Chaldea, Assyria, pp. 79, 80.
54. Ibid., I, "History of Ancient Egypt," pp. 150, 163.
55. Ibid., pp. 168, 169.
56. Ibid., pp. 187, 188.
57. Ibid., pp. 58, 169, 184; Lempriere, op. cit., pp. 132, 470; "An Encyclopedia of Freemasonry," by Albert G. Mackey, N. Y., 1900, pp. 242, 243, 577.
58. Mackey, op. cit., p. 288.
59. "Secret Destiny of America," by Manly Palmer Hall, Theosophical Research Society, Los Angeles, 1950, pp. 177-181.
60. Lempriere, op. cit., p. 561.
61. "The Encircled Serpent," by M. Oldfield Howey, David McKay Co., Philadelphia, 192-, pp. 17, 19.
62. Ibid., pp. 23, 25, 29-31.
63. Ibid., pp. 71, 72, 74, 76, 81, 84.
64. Mackey, op. cit., p. 137.
65. *Time Magazine*, April 4, 1955, p. 22, and March 5, 1956, p. 33; *New York Herald Tribune*, November 16, 1963, pp. 1, 2.

PART III

The Prayer Room In The United States Capitol

The Laymen's Movement's publication, *Christian Laymen*, May-June 1955, contained an article on the Prayer Room in the United States Capitol, which provided the information that Congressman Brooks Hays of Arkansas had attended a Laymen's Movement conference in 1952. He told the conference that he intended to introduce a resolution in Congress calling for the establishment of a prayer room in the Capitol. The Movement threw its weight behind the resolution and sent a mailing on the subject to 7500 of its Prayer Call supporters. An estimated 2500 letters to Congress resulted from this mailing. This pressure had its effect; opposition to the project was overcome in Congress. Weyman C. Huckabee, Secretary of the Movement, and Brooks Hays, were the first persons to use the facilities of the Prayer Room when it was opened in March 1955.

Senator Mike Monroney of Oklahoma introduced a companion resolution (Conc. Res. 14) to that offered by Congressman Hays (Conc. Res. 60), calling for the setting apart of a place for a prayer room (see The Prayer Room in the United States Capitol, House Document 234, 84th Congress, 1st Session). The Room is located on the House Side of the Capitol near the Rotunda. Delos H. Smith and Joseph W. Burcham, Architects of Washington, D.C., served as architectural consultants. "It was a first essential to make sure that no part of the furnishings and no symbol used would give offense to members of any church." To make certain that this did not occur an advisory panel was constituted, the members of which were the chaplains of the House and Senate, the Assistant Chancellor of the Archdiocese of Washington, and the Minister of the Washington Hebrew Congregation. "The furnishings, the window, and the symbols have met with the unanimous approval of the four."

According to the *Brooklyn Tablet*, April 2, 1955, "a scroll was eliminated from the original window design on the ground that it might have been regarded as a symbol" of a particular faith. The advisory group felt that "the decor should have a wholly non-denominational character." In spite of this advice, the two candelabra were placed on either side of the altar, even though they are traditionally associated with a specific faith.

The lighting in this meditation room is subdued. A concealed ceiling light focuses on the white oak altar, as in the U.N.'s room. There are ten chairs facing the altar, as in the U.N.'s room. "When illumined by the indirect lights of the shielded wall brackets, the room is a soft color symphony of blue and gold."

The stained glass window is cluttered and uninspiring. It was presented anonymously to the Prayer Room by the craftsmen in a studio in the Twenty-first Congressional District of California. Its central figure is that of the kneeling George Washington. In the medallion immediately surrounding the central figure, woven into the ruby glass, is the text from Psalm 16:1. Extending out from behind the figure are the four arms of one of the ancient forms of the Mystic Tau Cross: the X (see Part I).

The most striking feature of the entire window with its clutter of shapes and designs is the depiction of the reverse side of the Great Seal at the top of the medallion *above* the phrase from Lincoln's Gettysburg Address, "This Nation Under God." The obverse side of the Great Seal, with its Solomonic Crest, is at the bottom of the window.

The appearance of these occult symbols in such a religious setting, in the very heart of the Capitol, cannot be ascribed to chance. The direct participation of the Laymen's Movement in the establishment of the room provides a guarantee that the placement of the two sides of the Great Seal in the window was made with foreknowledge of their real meaning.

This window is described as "symbolizing our Nation at prayer" (H. Doc. 234, p. 3). It "speaks of that religious faith which has always been a part of the greatness of our Nation." The kneeling figure of Washington is placed there to remind us "of the words from his First Inaugural:

> ... it would be peculiarly improper to omit in this first official act, my fervent supplications to that Almighty Being who rules over the universe ..."

The two lower corners of the window each show the Holy Scriptures, an open book and a candle, signifying the light from God's law, "Thy Word is a lamp unto my feet and a light unto my path." Why was *this* particular quotation chosen? The terms "Word" and "light" have especially significant meanings in the occult lexicon. In the ancient mysteries of Egypt the Word "is said to have been the Tetragrammaton." (See source 9, Part I, p. 889.) "The connection of material light with ... mental illumination was prominently exhibited in all the ancient systems of religion and esoteric mysteries. Among the Egyptians ... the symbol of moral illumination ... was also the symbol of Osiris." (*Ibid.*, pp. 469-470.) These root-symbols are met with over and over again in all of the temples and designs used by the devotees of the "new" pagan cult.

[Persons involved in the establishment and decoration of the Prayer Room, in addition to those already named, were: the Senate Chaplain, Rev. Frederick Brown Harris; the House Chaplain, Rev. Bernard Braskamp; the Asst. Chancellor of the Archdiocese of Washington, Father Edward J. Herrmann; the Minister of the Washington Hebrew Congregation, Rabbi Norman Gerstenfeld; Representative Edgar W. Hiestand, who arranged for the gift of the mosaic window; Representatives Karl M. LeCompte of Iowa and Katharine St. George of New York, members of a committee which allegedly arranged for the design and equipment of the room; and the Architect of the Capitol, J. George Stewart. Representatives Hiestand and LeCompte are no longer in Congress.]

PART IV

The Temple Of Understanding

THE NEW HAMPSHIRE SUNDAY NEWS, MANCHESTER (N. H.) — Sunday, April 1, 1962

Between The Lines

The New Cult In Washington

By Edith Kermit Roosevelt

A temple will be erected in Washington, D. C., for "the citizen of the world" to develop "universal understanding" in place of his "nationalist limitations."

Planners for this $5 million edifice, called "The Temple of Understanding," say endorsers include Swami Prabhavananda of the Vedanda Society, Hollywood; Secretary of Defense Robert S. McNamara, Socialist leader Norman Thomas, Chester Bowles, special advisor to the President; Swami Bhaskaranand Paramhamsa of "UNISM," New Delhi, India; Thomas B. Watson, president of International Business Machines; Eleanor Roosevelt, the United Lodge of Theosophists, New York City, and others.

The futuristic building, characterized as a "spiritual UN" will be a "symbol of the brotherhood and sisterhood of mankind," according to the brochure issued from Temple headquarters, Greenwich, Conn. A wing of this modern-day Tower of Babel will be accorded to each of the six international faiths: Hinduism, Judaism, Buddhism, Confucianism, Christianity and Islam.

• • •

AMONG OTHER endorsers listed are Jack Benny, Douglas MacArthur II, ambassador to Japan: Max Lerner of the New York Post, Prof. J. B. Rhine of Duke University; Roland Gammon of the Laymen's Movement and World Parliament of Religions; Miguel Ydigoras Fuentes, president of Guatemala; Sir Roy Welensky, prime minister, Federation of Rhodesia and Nyasaland; Rev. Fred Jordan, president, International Spiritualists, Norfolk, Va.; Philip S. Linnik, director Universal Brotherhood Center, Glen Cove, Long Island, N. Y.; James A. Linen, president Time-Life Inc., and S. A. Mohamed, cultural attache of the United Arab Republic, Washington, D. C.

A "world publicity campaign" for donations is being launched. The names of the donors are to be enscribed on the stone walks of the temple.

• • •

THE SYMBOLISM planned for the building dates back to the black magic practiced by the high priests of ancient Egypt. The building will contain a giant eye — a circular pool of water which reflects light beamed onto it by a dome faceted to resemble a many-colored diamond. The temple brochure states:

"The dome will be illuminated all night in order to indicate, symbolically, that even while the world sleeps, the light of understanding continues to shine."

* * *

WHILE TEMPLE publicists proclaim the idea for the temple arose quite spontaneously out of a talk between two women friends, shrines for "the brotherhood of man" have been systematically used throughout history to create a mystique of collectivity.

Money was raised to build a similar shrine in London by the occultist, the late Mrs. Annie Besant. A sort of Eleanor Roosevelt of her day, Mrs. Besant worked closely with Nehru and Krishna Menon and was a founder of the Fabian Parliamentary League, a British socialist group in which Sidney Webb, Hubert Land, H. H. Champion and George Bernard Shaw were active.

* * *

MRS. BESANT'S temple featured six symbolic presentations of the six great international faiths in the lecture hall. Visiting "adepts" contemplated a mural of a six-pointed Theosophical star made of two interlocking triangles connected by a serpent.

This theme is repeated in the "Temple of Understanding." The brochure informs us that the temple's six wings "will contain the cultural facets of the 'diamond of truth.'"

* * *

IN NEW YORK CITY the "Friends of the Meditation Room" have long met regularly in the United Nations' Meditation Room. In the center of this shrine a beam of light plays on polished ore. On April 24, 1957, when the Meditation Room was reopened, the late Dag Hammarskjold, UN Secretary General, described this pagan stone as an altar to universal religion.

"The altar is the symbol of the God of all," he said.

The Temple of Understanding also will have its meditation room, to be known as the "Hall of Illumination." There, it is planned that the Illuminati, Masters of Wisdom, Our Leaders of the Temple of Understanding, will train the public in the new humanistic cult.

Meetings, film showings and courses of study in the world's great religions will be held in the "Hall of Illumination."

* * *

IT IS INTERESTING to note that for some time now a group who call themselves "the New Group of World Servers" have been holding "full moon meditation meetings" at the Carnegie Endowment International Centre in New York. On Dec. 21, 1961, this writer attended one of these meetings where pamphlets were distributed describing "the New World Religion." One "World Goodwill" booklet described what some of the backers of "The Temple of Understanding" may have in mind.

"A new type of mystic is coming to be recognized . . . he is distinguished by his lack of interest in his own personal development, by his ability to see God immanent in all faiths and not just in his own brand of religious beliefs."

* * *

WHERE THE internationalist would-be elite gather to plan and plot world government I heard a determined group of "World Servers" led by Foster Bailey chant in unison their eerie Great Invocation.

"Let purpose guide the little
wills of men—
"The purpose which the
Masters know and serve."

Is the real purpose of the world-minded Masters of Unism to guide and control us by pagan rites?

[Permission granted to reprint by Edith Kermit Roosevelt Syndicate Suite N 824, 800 Fourth St., S.W., Washington 24, D.C.]

THE NEW HAMPSHIRE SUNDAY NEWS, MANCHESTER (N. H.) — Sunday, October 21, 1962

Between The Lines

The Temple Of Understanding

By Edith Kermit Roosevelt

Unwrapping her gauzy veils a "White Madonna" danced on the podium. She symbolized "Christianity" or the "Mother of the World encompassing forms of the creative feminine spirit which has unfolded over centuries from Egypt, Babylonia, China and Europe," said a program distributed at the Temple of Understanding's benefit dinner.

The dinner, held Oct. 12 at the Waldorf Astoria, featured this dramatic skit on "Christianity" and five other skits on the major faiths to commemorate the $5,000,000 Temple to be built on 50 acres by the Potomac River, Washington, D. C.

The Temple brochure describes the edifice as a "Spiritual United Nations" designed to fulfill the rituals of the six major faiths and replace "nationalist limitations" with "universal understanding" for "citizens of the world!"

* * *

PUBLICISTS for this tax-exempt "Project Understanding" claim support from the "pennies donated by hairdressers, taxicab drivers and workers all over the world." But judging from the Temple's printed list of sponsors it can count on more influential backing. For instance:

John D. Rockefeller IV, Socialist leader Norman Thomas, Rt. Rev. James A. Pike of San Francisco, Cary Grant, Defense Secretary Robert S. McNamara, a founding member of the Fund for the Republic's Center for Democratic Institutions; militant pacifist and Nobel Peace Prize winner Philip Noel Baker; Holland D. Roberts of the Academic Freedom Committee, a former head of the Communist party's California Labor School who was identified as a "party member" at a Jan. 22, 1956 hearing of the Subversive Activities Control Board; U. Alexis Johnson, deputy undersecretary of state for political affairs; Sen. Kenneth B. Keating (R-N.Y.), Prof. Pitirim A. Sorokin, director of Harvard University's Research Center for Creative Altruism and Brooks Hays, special assistant to President Kennedy.

* * *

AT THE WALDORF'S Starlight Roof I heard Mrs. Dickerman Hollister, president of the Temple of Understanding (P. O. Box 191, Greenwich, Conn.), address some 500 UN delegates and socialites. In a voice choked with fervor, she said:

"We are seeding an idea to create a global symbol of the world."

Then she struck with a wand an egg held aloft by a child. Out popped a "magic" golden tree with six branches on either side.

* * *

THE SYMBOLISM is not surprising in view of the mystic appeal of the internationalist dream. For example, one of the Temple sponsors is Roland Gammon, former director of the Laymen's Movement, World Parliament of Religions. This international, non - sectarian group of big businessmen, psychiatrists and other professional men meet in the seclusion of Wainwright House, Milton Point, Rye, N. Y., to study scientific mind control.

I secured the texts of some of the Wainwright House seminars which treat of such topics as "clairvoyance," "automatic writing," "hallucinations," "religion as part of an enlarged science" and "the psychic content of the alchemical symbols."

According to this year's Sept.-Oct. issue of the Laymen's Review published at Wainwright House, the Movement "spearheaded" the establishment of the UN Meditations Room which happens to contain some of those "alchemical symbols."

* * *

THE UN MEDITATION Room mural is divided into 72 separate sections—the tetraggram'on or Divine Name of 72 w'rds. It depicts triangles and pyramids representing "the deity" in accordance with the ancient Babylonian symbols. Also a part of this mural is a spiral figure intertwining with a diagonal line which may represent Hermes' wand, the Cadeuces, traditional symbol of the sex forces or Kundalini.

The mural's center sphere and outer circle roughly form an eye. The "all seeing eye" of the deity theme is to be repeated in the Temple building by a glass eye faceted like a diamond to reflect the rays of the sun through the six wings.

* * *

IT IS INTERESTING to note that the Interparliamentary Union—Temple of Understanding sponsor Sen. Keating is IPU secretary—adopted a few weeks ago as its emblem: "A Temple of Law with six columns for the six continents to show the Universality of the Union." The IPU, which has been financed in part by the tax-exempt Carnegie Endowment for International Peace, consists of a training corps of legislators who meet regularly with their Communist "counterparts" to set up world parliamentary government.

* * *

WHILE SOME PEOPLE may dismiss these humanistic temples as another example of "goofy" internationalism, apologists for Moscow view them as a serious component in their drive to promote the "Social Gospel."

* * *

TWO TEMPLE sponsors are included in the Senate Internal Security's "list of the most typical sponsors of front organizations" published April 23, 1956. They are:

1. Jerome Davis, New Haven, Conn., educator who heads Promoting Enduring Peace, a group whose literature is distributed by the Arcane School (operated by the tax-exempt "non-political" Lucis Trust on the 32nd and 33rd floors of 11 W. 42nd St., N. Y.) The international Lucis Trust network, which has substantial financial backing, regularly holds "Full Moon Meditation Meetings" at the Carnegie Endowment for International Peace to promote UNESCO and the "New World Religion."

2. Prof. Kirtley Mather of the Geologic Museum, Cambridge, Mass., who has served on a 4-man panel evaluating "physical research" at Wainwright House.

* * *

ANOTHER TEMPLE backer is Rev. Lee H. Ball, executive secretary of the Methodist Federation for Social Action, an organization cited as a front by the Senate Internal Security Subcommittee on April 23, 1956. On July 7, 1953, Ben Gitlow, former secretary of the Communist party, testified under oath that Ball was one of "the principal individuals involved in the Communist conspiracy to subvert the church for Communist purposes."

Shouldn't they add the hammer and sickle symbol to the second "Meditation Room" slated for the new Washington Temple?

[Permission granted to reprint by Edith Kermit Roosevelt Syndicate Suite N 824, 800 Fourth St., S.W., Washington 24, D.C.]

THE TEMPLE — A "SPIRITUAL UNITED NATIONS"

Edith Kermit Roosevelt's marvelous columns on "The Temple of Understanding" focused nation-wide attention on this project for the erection of a "spiritual UN" in our Nation's Capitol. The Temple brochure referred to by Miss Roosevelt states (page 2) that each of the six wings radiating from the central dome of the Temple "will contain a small chapel which, designed in accordance with the requirements of the religion it represents, and using the appropriate symbols, will illustrate its mode of worship.

"To the right of each chapel, or wing, will be a combined library and reading room. The books in this adjacent library will cover the main currents of thought of the particular religion, including its various branches."

And, "beneath the main floor of the Temple . . . will be a Center of Understanding. . . . Here courses of study in the world's great religions will be given on both the student and layman level. . . . This downstairs area will serve children as well as adults and will be planned, acoustically, to protect the atmosphere of quiet in the great central Hall above."

In spite of the emphasis on religion as such in the description given above, the brochure contains a disclaimer: "The Temple is *not* to be used as a house of worship, but as an *educational edifice.*" (Emphasis supplied in brochure.) It also states that "in no way will this project, or those connected with it, seek to proselytize any one religion." Both of these statements need interpretation. A temple is an edifice dedicated to the service of a god. According to Curt John Witt, author of an article on the Temple reprinted from volume two, number one of *TRIAD* and "Main Currents of Modern Thought" (available at the Temple Information Center, 66 West Putnam Avenue, Greenwich, Connecticut; telephone TO 9-5054), "the upper level of the Temple of Understanding will center around a reflecting pool of water. This inner pool, surrounded by benches, will be designed *for meditation and prayer.* It will be kept completely quiet at all times, and be known as the 'Hall of Illumination.'" (Emphasis supplied.)

Is the Temple to be used as a place of worship or is it not? The statements cited are contradictory. Actually, common sense tells us that the intent of the Temple's founders is that religious worship shall be practiced in the building, but not in a form acceptable to any of the leaders of the world's great religions. Any claim *made at this time* by the backers of the Temple that it will indeed be a propaganda center and place of worship according to the tenets of a NEW WORLD RELIGION dedicated to the creation of a Universal Theocratic State would be unpalatable to the public and therefore premature. Edith Kermit Roosevelt has probed deeply into the make-up of the international apparatus which has been working to set up such a State. Her column on the subject dated October 28, 1962, follows:

BETWEEN THE LINES

by Edith Kermit Roosevelt

THE UNIVERSAL THEOCRATIC STATE

An international apparatus is working to set up a Universal Theocratic State.

Already the high priests, prayers and temples of the universal cult are with us. Curriculums are being drafted to indoctrinate our children in what John D. Rockefeller, Jr. calls "the church of all people."

The first step is to break down loyalty to a single religious faith. In June 1959 the Women's International Religious Fellowship (WIRF) was founded by representatives from 14 nations. This group composed of mothers of different faiths meet at bazaars and picnics so their children may share national dishes and learn the dances of foreign lands. Their meetings feature talks on Jainism, Taoism, Zoroastrianism, Hinduism, Sikhism and the five other major world faiths, according to literature distributed by WIRF headquarters, 1601 Webster St., N.W., Washington, D.C.

Participants in WIRF programs have included representatives from the embassies as well as Mrs. Marietta Tree, American delegate to the United Nation's Human Rights Commission.

Plans are being made to set up regional World Universities whose objectives would include "to instruct in all religions but will not make religion its aim," "build a world outlook" and "teach the physiological, psychological and spiritual aspects of sex."

John Howard Zitko, D.D., is coordinator of this World University Development Program (P.O. Box 68, Huntington Park, Calif.) He is also the author of a book on the *Lemurian Theo-Christian Conference* which warns that "advanced intelligences on other planets of our solar system are again becoming active in human affairs after a lapse of some ten thousand years."

Dr. Zitko's idea has received a boost from key World Leaders. On July 31, 1962 Dwight D. Eisenhower endorsed setting up a World University to provide "World Thinkers" to funnel into the United Nations. Carl F. Stover, director of science and technology at the Fund for the Republic's Center for Democratic Institutions, Santa Barbara, Calif., gave the principal address at Dr. Zitko's 15th World University Roundtable Conference on August 11 of this year. Incidentally, a founding member of the Santa Barbara Center is Defense Secretary Robert S. McNamara who along with Dr. Zitko is a sponsor of the Temple of Understanding, the $5,000,000 "Spiritual UN" for the six major faiths.

Like all world government projects the Temple's "Project of Understanding" just happens to coincide with a similar drive in Great Britain where fabian socialism was hatched under the wing of theosophy.

Implementing Britain's 1944 Education Act for teaching "comparative religion" a pilot project has been set up to take nine and ten-year-old children in a state school to hear informal talks by various ministers of different faiths.

The children were required to write essays on these interfaith experiences. The native exponents of Hinduism, Islam and Buddhism visited the school to further the cause of "east-west understanding." They lectured the students to "take their education in tolerance a step farther," reports London educator Bernard Cousin in the June, July, Aug., 1962 issue of the *Voice Universal*, chief organ for "Theocratic Union" (Published at 8 Watling Rd., Southwick, Brighton, Sussex, England.)

The Dec. 1961, Jan., Feb., 1962 issue of the *Voice Universal* features an international prayer or "Invocation of the United Nations," which our rulers may wish to substitute for the Christian prayers no longer permitted in our schools. It reads in part:

"May the Peace and the Blessing of the Holy Ones pour forth over the worlds – rest upon the United Nations, on the work and the workers . . .

"May the chalice the United Nations is building become a focal point for the descent of spiritual force . . .

"May the consciousness of the United Nations become ever more at-one, the many lights One Light in the Light of the Self."

Will the new Universal cult take root among the peoples of the world? If so, probably not for long. No faith based on man-made institutions can survive. Nevertheless, since the days of the "Mystic Temples" of the Greek Eleusinian mysteries "Wisdom" cults have been used as a means of recruitment for revolutionary groups as well as to influence politicians and statesmen at the highest level. Remember Rudolph Steiner and Kaiser Wilhelm and, more recently, former vice-president Henry A. Wallace and his guru Nicholas Roerich?

Recognizing the "goofy network" to be a source of power and influence, UN officials lecture at meetings of the Arcane School, the international "group of New World Servers," who form "Triangles" to work for UNESCO.

A few months ago Dr. Huston Smith, professor of philosophy at the Massachusetts Institute of Technology – a sponsor of the Temple of Understanding (P.O. Box 191, Greenwich, Conn.) – visited Sydney, Australia and lectured on "Is a New World Religion Coming" at the Blavatsky Lodge.

The name Blavatsky refers to the late Madame Helena Petrovna Blavatsky, the Russian cult leader known as "H.P.B." whose writings are used in the secret courses of instruction at the Arcane School (with offices at 11 W. 42nd St., New York 36, N. Y.)

In a moment of frankness, Madame Blavatsky explained the influence of magic on history:

"What is one to do, when in order to rule men, it is necessary to deceive them? . . . For almost invariably the more simple, the more silly, and the more gross the phenomenon, the more likely is it to succeed."

The reader will note, if he will examine the pictures of the models of the Temple on the back cover, that the building is constructed entirely according to a geometric pattern based on triangular and pyramidal forms. Even the "chapels" are triangular shaped, with the tip of the triangle cut off, as seen in all representations of the pyramid and the "floating eye." Viewed from above, the main building is constructed in the form of a six-pointed star, the symbol formed by two interlocking triangles, the Seal of Solomon.

Juliet Hollister,* author of a second article in *TRIAD* on the Temple, wrote that the Temple "should be of glass faceted like a diamond to let in all the sun, symbolic of the light of spiritual knowledge, and this in turn should be caught in a pool, so that within the very heart of the building, there would be a quiet focus of light. Even at night this diamond will glow and shine.... From this central dome will radiate six wings, like rays of the sun, each the home of one of the great living religions of the world." The pagan symbolism should not be lost to the reader. [*See as Judith elsewhere.]

Juliet Hollister,* equipped with the design of the Temple executed by the architect, Lathrop Douglas, approached Eleanor Roosevelt for her aid in planning the creation of the real Temple. She wrote that it was Mrs. Roosevelt "who suggested a trip around the world, in order to awaken the interest and enlist the support of religious leaders and heads of states."...Let the peoples of the world create this building, she said, and then it will belong to the whole world: It will be a Spiritual United Nations.

"This was the real beginning of our venture. I took Mrs. [Eleanor] Roosevelt's good advice; I visited our Embassy to the United Nations and I talked also with many other U.N. representatives. I went to Washington, and spent many hours in the State Department, in Senator [J. W.] Fulbright's office, the USIA, the Voice of America, and elsewhere."

Curt John Witt wrote that "the cultural center...below the upper (or religious) level of the building...will be for the use of the Washington Embassies.... It will be known as the 'Hall of Nations.'" The latest brochure issued by the Temple states that "land near the Great Falls of the Potomac ...is now being given by a generous donor. Here the building will be surrounded by an extensive park." Miss Margaret Johnson is the donor.

But why should this woman be allowed to donate this land for such a purpose? The House and Senate Committees on the District of Columbia headed by Representative John L. McMillan of South Carolina and Senator Alan Bible of Nevada have the power to deny the Temple's officers the right to erect such a pagan temple in the Nation's Capitol. Legislation can be originated to forbid such an enterprise. Hearings can be held which would allow the citizenry to be heard concerning this matter. The time to stop this project is *now* – before the Temple of Understanding becomes a reality. A national campaign to finance the Temple began on February 1, 1964.

The sponsors and backers of the Temple are many and powerful. The latest (1963) list of sponsors which is reprinted herein lists some 385 foreign endorsers and 1,375 Americans. The list is amazing. It contains *eight* American Ambassadors; *fourteen* Ambassadors to the United States; the Secretary of Defense of the United States, Robert Strange McNamara; Brooks Hays, Special Assistant to the President (associated with the Laymen's Movement and author of the resolution creating the Prayer Room); the Deputy Under Secretary of State for Political Affairs, U. Alexis Johnson; Assistant Secretary of State Robert F. Woodward; many Embassy, USAID, USIA, and other government officials; the President and Vice-President of India; other Presidents and Prime Ministers; the Buddhist Pope; members of the World Court; the Governors of Maryland and Oklahoma; Senators Kenneth Keating and John Sherman Cooper; the President of CBS News and the Vice-President of NBC; the President of *Time, Life, Inc.* and the President of the *Herald Tribune;* the President of Paramount Pictures; officials of the Theosophical Society, World Union, World Brotherhood, International Spiritualists, Vedanta Society, and the cited Fellowship of Reconciliation; identified members of the Communist Party and many long-time Communist-fronters (see E.K.R. columns); the head of the Socialist Party, Norman Thomas; financiers such as John D. Rockefeller IV; lawyers like Eustace Seligman of Sullivan and Cromwell; religious figures: Ralph W. Sockman, James A. Pike, Maurice N. Eisendrath, Henry P. Van Dusen, and Nelson Glueck; industrialists: Thomas B. Watson, Jr., President of IBM, and Milton Mumford, President, Lever Brothers; celebrities: Steve Allen, Arthur Godfrey, Jackie Robinson, Faith Baldwin, Jack Benny, Cary Grant, Garry Moore, and Pearl Buck; Mrs. Cyrus S. Eaton, wife of the foremost Soviet apologist in the United States; and hundreds of others.

The latest Temple leaflet, "Six Rays of Hope—," relates how Mrs. Dickerman (Judith-Juliet) Hollister received "unofficial" help for her Temple project from William Nims of the Ford Foundation (her first contact); Wallace Irwin of the State Department (who placed her project under the protection of the religious officers of the department); Dr. Frank Graham of the U.N.; Thomas Watson of IBM; Ernest Lee Jahncke of NBC; Samuel Pryor of Pan-Am Airways; Mrs. Ellsworth Bunker, wife of the American Ambassador to India (who named the project the "Temple of Understanding"); and Rabbi Israel Goldstein, former president of the World Jewish Congress (the first member of the board of directors of the Temple).

On February 5, 1964, a few days after the national campaign to publicize and finance the Temple began, President Lyndon B. Johnson spoke to the annual Presidential prayer breakfast at the Mayflower Hotel. Several Cabinet members were present. Chief Justice Earl Warren headed the group from the judiciary. President Johnson said that "a fitting memorial to the God that made us all" should be established in Washington. He asked the several hundred participants to take the lead in raising funds for a house of prayer that would be open to persons of all faiths at all times. (*N.Y. Times*, 2/6/64.) He did not make a *direct* reference to the Temple. Nevertheless, his statement was interpreted by Temple sponsors as pre-arranged support for their project, and as evidence of their immense influence in Washington.

INTERNATIONAL BOARD OF DIRECTORS

MRS. DICKERMAN HOLLISTER, President
LATHROP DOUGLASS, Vice-President
C. MARTIN WOOD, JR., Treasurer
MRS. ERNEST L. JAHNCKE, JR., Secretary
CURT JOHN WITT, Cultural Director

NORMA E. BOYD
RABBI ISRAEL GOLDSTEIN
MRS. W. M. Q. HALM
BISHOP SHINSHO HANAYAMA
SIR M. ZAFRULLA KHAN
MARY MACAULAY
REV. HARRY C. MESERVE
CHARLES J. MILLS
REV. WENDELL PHILLIPS
MRS. HAROLD RASMUSSEN
MAURICE M. ROSEN
RABBI SAMUEL SILVER
MRS. FREDERICK C. TANNER, JR.
DR. WEN YEN TSAO
MRS. MOHINI VASWANI
DR. T. K. VENKATESWARAN

EXECUTIVE COMMITTEE

MRS. DICKERMAN HOLLISTER, Chairman
LATHROP DOUGLASS
MRS. ERNEST L. JAHNCKE, JR.
CHARLES J. MILLS
MRS. HAROLD RASMUSSEN

WASHINGTON COMMITTEE

NORMA E. BOYD, Chairman
MRS. MOHINI VASWANI, Vice-Chairman
MRS. FLORENCE C. BACKUS
REV. G. L. FAUS
MRS. WILLIAM FELDMAN
JAMES V. GOURE
DOROTHY ORRISON
ROLAND I. PERUSSE
MRS. EUGENE O. SAPHIR
DR. LAURENCE C. STAPLES
DR. WEN YEN TSAO
MRS. SARAH ANN WADSWORTH

ARCHITECTURAL COMMITTEE

LATHROP DOUGLASS, Chairman
PHILIP JOHNSON

FINANCIAL COMMITTEE

C. MARTIN WOOD, JR., Chairman
MRS. E. L. JAHNCKE, JR.
CHARLES J. MILLS

CULTURAL COMMITTEE

CURT JOHN WITT, Chairman
MAULSBY KIMBALL
DR. RAYMOND PIPER
DR. PITIRIM A. SOROKIN
DR. STEPHEN TORNAY
DR. ALFRED UHLER

STUDENT COMMITTEE

PATRICIA BINKERD, Chairman
JEFFREY REYNOLDS, Vice-Chairman
CATHARINE de RAPALYE HOLLISTER Secretary
CHRISTOPHER SHAW
AMANDA MORTIMER
MARJORIE REYNOLDS
G. CLAY HOLLISTER
PAMELA PERKINS
JOHN SYZ

LIST OF SPONSORS

Algeria
Marcel Belaiche, World Brotherhood

Argentina
Dr. Victor M. Mosquera, Director, Psychologiae Studium • Dr. Francisco A. Propato, Chairman, World University Roundtable, Buenos Aires • Nazareno E. Rimini

Australia
Regional Head:
Mrs. Ethel Taylor
"Devon", 91 Patrick St., Hobart, Tasmania
Steven Carley • Michael Duggan • Vincent C. Fairfax, Chief Commissioner for New South Wales Boy Scouts of Australia • Gladys Evelyn Heinicke • Mrs. Natalie Jackson • Charles F. Knight, President, Buddhist Society of New South Wales • Patricia Mallon • Dorothy Meyer • Mrs. Helen F. Moyes • A. Panayotis • Norris Pierson, Vacuum Oil Company, Melbourne • Dr. Arthur Reicher • B. Roberts • The Honorable William J. Sebold, Ambassador, Embassy of the United States of America • Peter White, "Havilah"

Austria
Dr. Kurt J. Offenberger

Belgium
Mme. Tilla Grenier • The Honorable Douglas MacArthur, II, Ambassador, Embassy of the United States of America • Countess Alwina van Limburg-Stirum • Countess Aurelie van Limburg-Stirum

Brazil
Robert J. Poor • Atlantic Refining Company • George Craig Smith • Countess Violette Vorontzov-Daschkov

Burma
A. Khalique

Canada
Mrs. Howard Austin, Jr. • Mrs. Winifred Banville • His Grace, The Most Reverend Dr. Odo Barry • Mrs. Odo Barry • C. L. Bell • Mrs. Dorothy Brisley • Jessie C. Burnett • Mrs. Carlson • David R. M. Chapman, University of McGill • His Excellency, F. S. Chu, Minister, Embassy of The Republic of China • Mrs. Katherine De La Franier • Miss S. G. Ferguson • The Reverend W. A. Glazer • E. W. Gordon • Mrs. M. B. Hamilton • Marion Hescott • F. Levasseur • Mrs. Elizabeth Marquardt • Gordon E. Matthews, Headmaster, Agnes G. Hodge Public School • Edna Mayhew • Mrs. Katherine D. Paddington • Mrs. R. G. Powers • Mrs. B. D. Rachlin • Mrs. W. D. Tucker, President "Voice of Women"

Ceylon
Her Excellency, Sirimavo Bandaranaike, Prime Minister of Ceylon • Mr. and Mrs. E. D. F. Cooray • His Excellency, W. Dahanayake, Former Prime Minister of Ceylon • Dr. W. S. Fernando, Principal, The Universal College of Panadura • A. Hector De Zoysa • K. Ramachandra • Dr. Johnson Thambimuttu • The Reverend Akuralea W. Tissa

Republic of China
Dr. Chi-Yun Chang, Director, The Institute of Chinese Culture, Taiwan • Mr. and Mrs. Wesley C. Haraldson, U.S.A.I.D. • Mr. and Mrs. Bernard J. Oliver, U.S.A.I.D. • Mr. and Mrs. Clarence Sondern, U.S.A.I.D. • Mr. and Mrs. Frank Tessitor, U.S.A.I.D.

Cuba
Dr. Jose T. Fernandez Jane

Czechoslovakia
The Honorable Edward T. Walles, Ambassador, Embassy of The United States of America

Denmark
Dr. and Mrs. Klaus Jensen

Ecuador
His Excellency, Camilo Ponce Enriquez, Former President of Ecuador

France
Regional Head:
Welles Bosworth, F.A.I.A.,
"Villa Marietta", Vaucresson, Seine et Oise, France
Monsieur et Madame Henri E. Boitel • Mrs. Welles Bosworth • Monsieur et Madame Robert de Witt • Mr. and Mrs. Lewis Einstein, Embassy of The United States of America • Mr. and Mrs. Frederick Feldkamp • The Honorable Thomas K. Finletter, U.S. Permanent Representative on the North Atlantic Council • Ian Forbes Fraser, President, American Library of Paris • The Honorable Johnson Garret, Ass't. Sec. General of Procurement and Logistics for N.A.T.O. • Mrs. Johnson Garret • Harvey S. Gerry, Vice President, National City Bank of New York, Paris • Mrs. Harvey S. Gerry • Mrs. John G. Gossett • John Gossett, Jr. • M. Greber • Morris Hughes, First Consul, Embassy of The United States of America • Isabelle Kamp • Mr. and Mrs. Joseph Verner Reed • The Very Reverend Sturgis Riddle, Dean, The American Cathedral of Paris • Madame A. Sepeque

Federal German Republic
Lynne Gossett, Munich Branch of The University of Maryland • Professor Gollwitzer, University, West Berlin • Dr. Frederich Heiler, University of Marburg • Frau Johanna Hirth • Frau Margaret Johndorff • Professor Rasenberger-Koch, General Secretary, World Parliament for World Culture • Dr. Med. Siegmund Schmidt • Walther Schulz • Ulrich Weissenberg

Ghana, West Africa
Regional Head:
Mrs. W. M. Q. Halm
Accra, Ghana, West Africa
J. F. Acquaye • C. A. Aidoo • K. Brakatu Ateko • S. B. Ayitey-Adjin • Robert Dodoo, General Manager, Methodist Schools • The Reverend F. C. F. Grant, Methodist Church • Honorable W. M. Q. Halm, Former Ambassador to The United States of America • The Reverend T. W. Koomson, Methodist Mission • The Honorable Francis H. Russell, Ambassador, Embassy of The United States of America • J. Antubam Sackey • Mrs. Christina Tetteh

Great Britain
Regional Head:
Mary Macaulay
10 Exhibition Road, London S.W. 7, England
Joan Allen • Dr. Lydia Torrence Allen • Mrs. Arkwright • Dr. and Mrs. George Arnsby Jones • Mrs. Monica Askey • Tony Astley • Frances Banks • Maurice Barbanell • Sri A. Basu, Spalding Lecturer, University of Durham • Mrs. John Bendall, • Dr. and Mrs. L. J. Bendit • Mrs. Audrey Beste • Heather Beste • Gaye Beste • Mrs. Doris Black • Mr. and Mrs. Bowdler • Mr. and Mrs. Bowman • Albert Bowman • His Grace, The Most Reverend Brearley • Mr. and Mrs. E. Tease Browne • Grace M. Burton • Joseph Busby • Mrs. Constance Buttenshaw • Judith Carr, The House of Citizenship, Cambridge • Mohamed Ali C. Chagla, High Commissioner of India • Lt. Col. and Mrs. R. M. Chapman • Sir Robert and Lady Chapman • Lillian E. Clark • Mrs. Gordon Clemetson, Editor-in-Chief, "Kent and Sussex Courier" • Mr. and Mrs. Conrad • Harry Dawson •

Herbert Dove • Winifred Elin • George Farquharson • Mrs. A. C. W. Ferguson • Mrs. Doris Girling • Mrs. Alice Gilbert, President, World Spiritual Council • Philip Gilbert • Captain James Goodwin • Reverend Dr. J. P. Grant • Kenneth Grant • Grete Greenfield • Miss M. V. Grigg • His Excellency R. S. S. Gunewardene, High Commissioner for Ceylon in Britain • Grace Hall • Andrew Hamer • Captain and Mrs. Douglas Harrison • Mr. and Mrs. Talbert Hills • Mrs. Kathleen Hines • Ann Hodgson • Norman Hoyte • Dr. Colette Inebnit • Dr. Martin Israel • R. Ahmad Jalandri • Mr. D. H. Josef • Mrs. I. C. Kemp • Star Kosiar • Alice Laurie • Mrs. Legh, O.B.E., J.P. • Jennifer Lunn • Kathleen MacVitie • Mrs. Nancy Magor • Mrs. Guy Mansell • Mrs. Marion Mathias • Sir Robert Mayer, World Brotherhood, London • Iris McIntosh • Mrs. Robert C. McMullin • Len Mellows • Mrs. A. M. Mobbs • Frederick Molz • Mr. and Mrs. Maurice Moon • Mrs. Dorothy R. Morgan • Maud Nevill • The Right Honourable Philip Noel-Baker, Nobel Prize For Peace, 1959 • Roland Northover • Swami Bhaskaranand Paramhamsa, "Unism" • The Reverend John Rowland • Jane Oliver • The Reverend George Parkinson • Lydia Parks • Patricia Paterson • Phyllis Pearson • Mrs. Joan M. Phillips • Mrs. Rowena Phillips • Mr. and Mrs. Torrey Pilgrim • G. Jafar Qasimi, Islamic Cultural Center & London Mosque • Evelym Raemaekens • James Raglan • Mr. and Mrs. L. Rampton, Theocratic Union • Mrs. Eleanor Road • Mrs. K. A. Robertson • Mrs. Ralph Rossiter • S. K. Sakhuja • Mrs. Helen Salter • David Salzedo • Mrs. Richard A. Sanders • Arthur Skinner • Winefred Slade • John Snow, Chairman, The Caravan of Great Britain • Mr. and Mrs. Edwin Spencer • Mrs. Florence Surgey • Mrs. E. M. Thomas • Peg Ticehurst • Barbara Ventress • Mrs. Irma Ward • Miss L. E. Wheeler • Mr. and Mrs. C. H. Williams • Mrs. M. E. Williams • Freda Wood • World Congress of Faiths, London

Republic of Guatemala

Miguel Ydigoras Fuentes, President of Guatemala

Republic of Guinea

The Honorable William Attwood, Ambassador, Embassy of The United States of America

Hong Kong, B.C.C.

Dr. Irene Cheng • Tank Chun, I, Dean, New Asia College • Professor F. S. Drake, University of Hong Kong • R. B. Kramers, Head of Buddhist Christian Mission • P. M. Liu, University of Hong Kong • James Robinson, N.B.C. News • Professor Mou Tsung San, Philosophy Department, New Asia College • Chen Chao Shung, Dean of Students, New Asia College • Mrs. Tseng To • Professor Hsien Tse-Yu, Dean, Institute of Advanced Chinese Studies of New Asia College • Dr. Arthur W. Woo • Wong Tao • Shumwai Yau, Editor, Overseas Chinese Daily News • Wong Yuk

India

Regional Head:
B. K. Birla
"Birla House," Calcutta,. India

Mrs. Atiya Ansari • Dr. B. Bagchee • M. L. Bagrodia • Mr. M. L. Bagrodia Rusi D. Banaji • Swami Bhaskaranand Paramhamsa • Aditya Birla • G. D. Birla • Mr. Shyam Das • His Excellency V. V. Giri, Governor of Kerala • B. D. Goenka, Director, Express Newspapers Private, Ltd. • P. C. Goyal, Commissioner of Income Tax • Sri Purushottamdass Halwasiya • Dr. Zakir Hussain, Vice-President of India • Rajkumari Amrit Kaur, Member of Parliament • K. K. Khemka • Dr. G. Kohli, "Humanitarian Mission" • Eleanor Lapsley, Isabella Fholuen College, Lucknow, U.P. • Marguerite Lidchi, World Union International Centre • Swami B. H. Bon Maharaj, Institute of Oriental Philosophy • Sami Ullah Mekrany • Mihir K. Mukerji • M. N. Mukherji • His Excellency Dr. K. M. Munchi, Governor, Uttar Pradesh State • His Highness Jaya Chamarja Wadiyar, Maharaja of Mysore • R. Narayanswamy • His Excellency, Moekarto Notowidigdo, Embassy of Indonesia • A. B. Patel, Vice-President of World Union • His Highness Maharaja of Patiala • Mr. and Mrs. J. K. Paul • Swami Premananda • Dr. Sarvepalli Radhakrishnan, President of India • Sri Charat Ram • Sri N. Ram, President Theosophical Society • John T. Reid, Cultural Attache, United States Information Service. • Swami Saswatananda, Belur Math, Ramakrishna Mission • Brigadier Raj Sarin • V. P. Sharda • Yuvraj Karan Singh, Maharaja and Governor of Jamma and Kashmir State • Dr. Jay Holmes Smith, General Secretary, World Union • H. R. Sugla • J. R. D. Tata, Tata Industries, Ltd.

Indonesia

Betty Liem Soen Nio • His Excellency Sri Apa B. Pant, Ambassador, Embassy of India • Maha Upasaka A. Surya • Mr. and Mrs. O. W. Wassmer

Iran

Shah Mohammed Riza Pahlevi • Jaffa Sharif-Imami, Prime Minister of Iran

Iraq

Brigadier General Abdul Karim Kassim • Brigadier General Nadim Rubaiya, President, Baghdad Council • The Honorable John D. Jernegan, Ambassador, Embassy of The United States of America

Israel

Regional Head:
Rabbi Israel Goldstein
The Executive of the Jewish Agency, Jerusalem, Israel

Yitzhak Ben-Zvi, President of Israel • Mr. Shalom Ben-Chorin • Dr. Hugo Boyko, Secretary-General, World Academy of Art & Science • Hans Zeuger, General Secretary, Theosophical Society

Italy

Vernon Bartlett, C.B.E., • Mr. and Mrs. Edward Bayne • Professor Ermanio Leonide Clemente • Luigi La Sala • Landon K. Thorne, Jr. • Prince Ugo G. Tomassini-Paterno • Angelo G. Sciolari • Miles K. Wood

Japan

Regional Head:
Tenko Nishida
The Itto-En, Yamashima, Kyoto, Japan

Professor Tetsutaro Ariga, Professor of Christianity, Kyoto University • Mr. and Mrs. Cecil Brown, N.B.C. Foreign Correspondent, Tokyo • Mrs. Sumi Hirose, President, Kotobuki Tochi Co., Ltd. • H. S. Hisamatsu, Zen Buddhist Leader • Keisuke Ishiwawa, Secretary General of United Nations Association • Yoshijiro Ishikawa • Ami Kazai, Head Shinto Priest of Japan • The Reverend Kyoshin Kitabatake • Takashi Komatsu, President, The America-Japan Society • Toraji Makino, Hon. Citizen of Kyoto • Miss E. Rotty • Mr. and Mrs. Setsuzo Sawada, World Brotherhood, Tokyo • Archbishop Rosen Takashina • Fumiyasu Takizawa • Masaharu Taniguchi, Founder of the Seicho-no-ie • Mr. and Mrs. James M. Tompkins, American International Underwriters Japan, Inc. • William P. Woodard, Director of Research at the "International Institute for the Study of Religions"

Jordan

Priest Abed M.S. Samri, Samaritan

Kenya

Kuldeep Uppal

Liberia

Honorable George A. Padmore, State Department, c/o Department of State, Monrovia, Liberia

Federation of Malaya

Al Helmy Burhanuddin, President, Pan Malaya Islamic Party • Dr. Dali Muin, Malaysia Health Centre • Dr. C. H. Yeang

Mauritius

Meernaidoo Thodi Somanah

Mexico

George K. Hundley, American Friends Service Committee

Morocco

Abdullah Ibrahim, Former Prime Minister • Colonel Serge S. Boulatzel

Natal, South Africa

Klauspeter Langheim, Paramhansa Yogananda Trusts

Nepal

B. P. Koirala, Former Prime Minister of Nepal

The Netherlands

R. J. Advocaat • Mr. and Mrs. H. E. Kuipers • Jan van der Linden • Countess Louise van Limburg-Stirum • Mrs. P. Th Wassmer • Judge V. K. Wellington Koo, The International Court of Justice, The Hague

New Zealand

Regional Head:
Richard St. Barbe Baker
Mount Cook Station, P.O. Fairlie, New Zealand

Mrs. Estelle E. Aird • K. J. Edney • Alexander Hall • R. D. Mack • Harold Maude • Honorable Walter Nash, Former Prime Minister of New Zealand • Mr. and Mrs. H. W. Powell • Charles Williams, Member, Board of Directors of Waitangi National Trust Co. • S. D. Reeves, President, Federated Farmers of New Zealand

Nigeria, West Africa

Dr. Samuel Ontinwa Ogunloye

Pakistan

Syed Hamde Ali • Mrs. M. S. Shaikh, Ministry of External Affairs • Mrs. G. E. Minualla

Panama Canal Zone

Mrs. John W. Muller

Republic of The Philippines

Honorable Carlos P. Garcia, Former President of The Republic of the Philippines • Honorable Carlos P. Romulo, President, University of The Philippines

Poland

Conrad Strzelczyk Sphinx

Puerto Rico

Mrs. J. S. Becker • Robert Brank Fulton, Inter-American University

Southern Rhodesia

Nathan Shamuyarira, Africa Newspapers, Ltd. • Sir Roy Welensky, Prime Minister of the Federation of Rhodesia and Nyasaland • Paul Zimba

Spain

Dr. V. L. Ferrandir • Guy Murchie

Sweden

Alfred le S. Jenkins, Counselor of the Embassy of The United States of America • The Honorable J. Graham Parsons, Ambassador, Embassy of The United States of America

Switzerland

Professor Hans Casparis, President, Albert Schweitzer College • Peter G. Duker • Mr. and Mrs. Hemmi • M. Arthur Leuba • Victor Loeb, World Brotherhood • Eberhardt Reinhardt, World Brotherhood • Arthur Sachs

Thailand

Regional Head:
Adam W. Aitken
Thorensen Bldg., Suriwongse Road, Bangkok, Thailand

Princess Prem • Sondej Pramah Veerawong, Buddhist Pope • Prince Wan Waithayakon, Deputy Prime Minister of Thailand

Trinidad

Samuel Cozier • James Gray • Dr. Andrew T. Choy-Lee • Umilta Ramsay

Turkey

Dr. E. Ranos • Senator Ali S. H. Urguplu, President of the Senate

United Arab Republic

Mohammed Abdullah el Araby, Professor Law Faculty, Cairo University • Professor Mohammed Fahmy Mohammed Awad, International Muslim

Journalist • John E. Goodridge, Manager, First National City Bank of New York, Cairo Branch • Mahmood Shaltout, Rector of Azhar University • Aly Abdel Rahman el Kholy, Egyptologist, Cairo University • Anwar el Sadat, Secretary — General Islamic Congress • Pierre Stonborough, First National City Bank

Union of South Africa

Mrs. Betty Myburgh • Paramhansa Yogananda Ashram • Paramhansa Yogananda Meditation Shrine • Mrs. Mary G. Patterson • Mrs. F. G. Thompson • Mrs. Nel van Schalkwyk

UNITED STATES OF AMERICA

Alabama

Ambassador Clare H. Timberlake, State Dep't. Advisor, Air University, United States Air Force

Arizona

Dr. and Mrs. Hiram S. Davis • Columba Krebs • Dr. Margaret Sanger, LL.D., President Emeritus, International Planned Parenthood Federation

California

Regional Heads:

Mrs. Gladys Herbekian,
1406 Brinkley Ave., Los Angeles, Calif.

G. Zeth Brooks,
211 North Main St., Elsinore, Calif.

Mrs. James Boswell,
835 Black Mountain, Hillsborough, Calif.

Jeanne Adriel • Eddie Albert • Steve Allen • Mrs. Gladys E. Le Grand Baker • Harry Baker • Mr. and Mrs. Larry Barretto • The Very Rev. C. Julian Bartlett, Dean, Grace Cathedral, San Francisco • Mrs. C. Julian Bartlett • Mrs. J. Beaulieu • Mrs. Helen Bell • Jack Benny • S. L. Berry • Mrs. Wilna I. Black • William Blowitz • Mrs. Sarah F. Bordman • Rosa Lee Boswell • Mrs. Anton Bratburg • Mr. and Mrs. V. L. Bressie • Mr. and Mrs. Elbert Bressie • Mrs. Frank Broback • F. R. Brooks • Spring Byington • Mr. and Mrs. Coleman E. Campbell • Katie Cavanagh, Stamford University • Josephine Chambers • Haridas Chaudhuri, President Cultural Integration Fellowship • Mrs. Marie Clapper • Ruth E. Clark • Mrs. Darlene Cochran • Rev. Walton E. Cole, Unitarian Society of Pomona Valley • Lenore Cook • Mrs. Wilbur C. Cook • Mr. and Mrs. Spencer V. Cortelyou • Mrs. Wallace Crowe • Mr. and Mrs. C. V. Cunningham • Clara T. Donatoni • Mr. and Mrs. Philip Drath • Mrs. J. Duncan Dyer • Mrs. Robert Faust • Jerome Feig • Mr. and Mrs. Guido Ferrando • Flavia Flavin • Mr. and Mrs. Martin Flavin • Nathan J. Friedman • Mrs. Marlcia Fuerst • Mr. and Mrs. R. C. Gooding • Cary Grant • Mrs. Mary Green • Marjorie J. Greer • Mrs. Alice M. Hamilton • Dr. Shinsho Hanayama, Bishop, Buddhist Churches of America • Benjamin Harris • Mrs. Warwick Hayes • Dr. Ernest Heckler • Mr. and Mrs. P. B. Hitchcock • Mrs. Lois Holmes • Thelma Horwitz • Mrs. Dana Howard • Dr. Trevor Hoy, Canon, Grace Cathedral, San Francisco • Dr. Allen A. Hunter • Mr. and Mrs. Willis B. Hunting, Institute of International Relations, Stanford University • Christopher Isherwood • Jill Jackson • Leila Jahncke, Stanford University • Nancy D. Jaster • Carolyn A. John • Dr. Abraham Kaplan, University of California at Los Angeles • Mrs. D. Kasparian • Mrs. Frederic V. Kayser • Sonya Keller • Mrs. Ruth Kellogg • Mrs. Virginia Kellog • Nat Ketcham • Mrs. Clement M. Key • Willis H. Kinnear • Mrs. Julie Laviguer • Dr. and Mrs. Hyman Lischner • Jewel J. Littlejohn • Dr. E. Loomis • Winnifred MacGowan • Sri Daya Mata • Murdoch Matheson • Mrs. Eleanor Wilson McAdoo • Ethel McDonald Charles M. McIntosh • Mrs. A. Marfian • Jean Merritt • Betty Merritt • Mrs. Bruce Milne • Vivian Minton • Mrs. E. B. Newman • Richard Allan Newman • Mrs. Joyce Newton • E. Ray Nichols, Jr. • Mr. and Mrs. Alfred O'Day • Mrs. Mary Olds • Dr. and Mrs. Charles Oliver • Mr. and Mrs. Charles Paulsen • Mrs. Elsie E. Pearson • The Rt. Rev. James A. Pike, Bishop, Diocese of California • Swami Prabhavananda, Vedanta Society of Southern California • Mr. and Mrs. Alfred Stuart Pratt • Rev. L. E. Rider • Holland Roberts, Academic Freedom Committee • Mr. and Mrs. Frederick H. Rompage • Ruth Rontsony • Brother Rothman • Edith Mason Rowe, International Arts Foundation • Beulah H. Rynerson • Mrs. Jeanne Sapp • Dorothy L. Schindler • Dorothy Schmidt • Rev. and Mrs. Harry B. Scholefield, Unitarian Church, San Francisco • Mrs. Adine Sklabinsky • Mrs. Ben Snyder • Mr. and Mrs. Harry Spoon • Mrs. S. C. Stengel • Mrs. Frederick L. Stephens • Mrs. Paul Sterner • Mrs. Herbert Stevens • Mr. Leland P. Stewart, Executive Director, Peace Centers Foundation, Inc. • Mrs. R. H. Storm • Mr. and Mrs. Grant Theis • Mr. and Mrs. Paul F.Thiele • Rev. Irving C. Tipton, Princeton Methodist Church • Hope Troxell • Dr. Judith M. Tyberg, East-West Cultural Center • Rachel M. Van Ess • Aurele Vermeulen • Myrtle Weese • Dr. Frederick H. Werth • Otto Wilhelm • Mrs. Rosemary Williams • Henry Winchester • Rev. Edward Worcester • Cabot Yerxa • Fern Zimmerman • Dr. Howard John Zitko, World University Roundtable, Intn'l Secretariat • Mrs. Jean Zumbrun • Dr. and Mrs. A. Zwickel

Colorado

Hal J. Jennings • Professor and Mrs. Duncan MacEwen • Patricia Yingst

Connecticut

Mr. and Mrs. Braman B. Adams, Adams and Peck, New York • George B. Agnew, Jr. • Mrs. Vincent Andrus • Mrs. Watson Armitage • Mr. and Mrs. Edward C. Armstrong, Senior Vice-Pres., Union New Haven Trust Company • Robert G. Arnold • Norman Artus • Mrs. Edwin Bacon • Mrs. Cathe Baier • Mr. and Mrs. Frederick H. Baird • Mrs. D. Harvey Baker • Mr. and Mrs. David S. Baker, Jr. • Faith Baldwin • Mr. and Mrs. W. H. Baldwin • Mrs. Helen Morgan Ballantine • Mr. and Mrs. David Ballou • Frederick D. Ballou, II • Peter Ballou • Mrs. Kendall M. Barney • Edward W. Barrett, Dean, School of Journalism, Columbia University • Mrs. Farris Barry • Rev. C. Gordon Beale, Second Congregational Church, Greenwich • Mr. and Mrs. Harry Behn • George P. Bent, II • Mr. and Mrs. Richard Billings • Alan Binkerd • Mr. and Mrs. Alfred Binkerd • Mrs. R. F. Bishop • William B. Blood • Mrs. Hilya Brigadier • Mr. and Mrs. Vincent J. Brosnahan • Laura Bucknell • Mrs. Roger H. Bullard • Mr. and Mrs. Richard Burdett • Mr. and Mrs. Alan Burnham • Mr. and Mrs. John L. Burns • Rev. Raymond E. Burns, Albertson Memorial Church • Betty Bussman • Mr. and Mrs. Charles M. Butler • Mrs. Leonard Butler • Paul Butterworth • Richard P. Buzzio • Mrs. David Calhoun • Ruth West Campbell • Helen Carr • Dean and Mrs. Richard C. Carroll, Yale University • Mrs. Lawrence W. Carstensen • Mrs. John Fletcher Caskey • Mrs. Barbara K. Caturani • Robert Chavar • Mrs. Colby M. Chester, III • Mr. and Mrs. Nigel Cholmeley-Jones • Dr. Tibor de Cholnoky, National President, Hungarian Relief, • Mrs. Erwin T. Clark • Walter Houston Clark • Mr. and Mrs. William Clark • Mr. and Mrs. B. W. Clarke, Jr. • Mr. and Mrs. Donald Cleveland • Mrs. F. Stanley Clulow • Bud Collyer • Marjorie Campbell Cooke, Associate Editor, "Women Speaking" • Mrs. Hedessa Wickett Cordley • Mrs. Judson L. Cross • Mrs. Gerald Cunningham • Mr. and Mrs. Daniel B. Curll • Mr. and Mrs. L. Jarvis Cushing, Jr. • Rabbi Moshe Davidowitz, Temple Sholom, Greenwich • Mrs. Albert H. Davis, II • Dr. Jerome Davis, Promoting Enduring Peace, Inc. • Mr. and Mrs. Huntington T. Day, Wiggin and Dana, New Haven • Dr. and Mrs. Stanley R. Dean • Vivian de Marco • Mr. and Mrs. Richard Deutsch • Mrs. Gilbert E. Donahue • Mr. and Mrs. William J. Donnelly • Mrs. Lathrop Douglass • Mrs. Edward Duble • Mrs. Rhett du Pont • Mrs. Soutter Edger • Bennett Edson • Mrs. R. C. Edson • Rabbi Joseph H. Ehrenkranz, Congregation Agudath Sholom, Stamford • Katherine Ekert • Mr. and Mrs. Alanson T. Enos, III • Mr. and Mrs. Adrian M. Farley, Jr. • Mrs. Roscoe Kent Fawcett • Mrs. William Felck • Isabelle Ferguson • Mrs. F. H. Filley • Mr. and Mrs. Everett Fisher • Dr. D. H. Fogel • Michael W. Freeland • Jody Futtner • Mr. and Mrs. John Gabriel • Helen M. Gail • Mr. and Mrs. Benjamin T. Gaillard • Rev. Cecil D. Gallup, First Baptist Church, Greenwich • Garret J. Garretson, II, Vice-President, Turner Halsey Company, New York • Mrs. James Garretson • Mrs. Margaret M. Gerard • Mrs. F. M. Garrigue • John E. Gerli, Vice President, Palmer Engine Company • Mary A. Geyer • Mrs. Rena Gist • Rev. T. W. Graham, First Presbyterian Church, Greenwich • Mrs. Zuleika L. Ginesi • Richard Glock • Mrs. Julian C. Gonzalez • Mr. and Mrs. Henry Groh • William Harms • Rev. John J. Hawkins, St. Paul's Episcopal Church, Riverside • Mrs. Dennis Hendricks • Mr. and Mrs. Robert W. Hersey • Mrs. Thomas D. Hewitt • Mrs. Warren E. Hoagland • Mrs. Charles Hoddinott • Mrs. Richard Wallace Hogue • Mr. and Mrs. John Hohlstein • Dickerman Hollister, Jr. • Mr. and Mrs. Frank E. House, Jr. • Mrs. Laura M. Hunter • Mrs. Arnold T. Hutcheson • Werner H. Isaacs • Mr. and Mrs. John S. Jackson • Dr. and Mrs. Charles E. Jacobson, Jr. • Ernest L. Jahncke, Jr., Vice President, National Broadcasting Company, New York • Mrs. Philip C. Jessup • Carolyn A. John • Mrs. Edwin H. Johnson • Roy W. Johnson • Mr. and Mrs. Graham T. Johnston • Dr. Robert M. Kane • Mrs. Henry P. Kennedy • Richard Kernochan • Dr. Isabelle MacDonald Kerr • Emily N. Kimball • Richard King, President, Electric Indicator Company, Stamford • Mr. and Mrs. Harry Kleinert • Mr. and Mrs. Harold Kusen • Ethel Kweskin • Mrs. Edwin C. Laird • J. Carvel Lange, Economic Adviser to Time, Life and Fortune Magazines, New York • Mrs. J. Carvel Lange • Mrs. Frank Y. Larkin • Ottilie Lentes • Mrs. C. Pendleton Lewis • Mr. and Mrs. Paul Linz • Albert A. List, Chairman of the Board, Albert A. List Foundation, Inc. • Mr. and Mrs. Robert C. Livingston • Dr. Jane Lockwood • Dr. and Mrs. W. Farnsworth Loomis • Rev. Sidney Lovett, Chaplain Emeritus, Yale University • Mr. and Mrs. William Lowe • Rev. and Mrs. Douglas H. Loweth • Mr. and Mrs. W. Stuart MacFarlaine • Nicholas Manero • Mrs. Charles Alexander Marshall • Mr. and Mrs. Frank Marzullo • Mr. and Mrs. Frank Marzullo, Jr. • Mr. and Mrs. Joseph Marzullo • Mr. and Mrs. Charles P. Mason • Katinka Matson • Mr. and Mrs. J. Gardiner McAnerney • David McCabe • Mr. and Mrs. William McClennan • Mrs. Alfred McCormack • Mr. and Mrs. Jacques Mejean, Exec. Vice President, Aerotec Industries, Inc. • Paul Mejean • Curtis G. Mellen • John Merchant • Mr. and Mrs. Edward W. Miller • Erika Miller • Rev. and Mrs. Payson Miller, First Unitarian Congregational Society, Hartford • Mr. and Mrs. Edward E. Mills, President, Longmans, Green and Company, New York • Mr. and Mrs. Lamont Moore • Albert P. Morano, Former Congressman • Mrs. Madeline Mueller • Mr. and Mrs. Alvin W. Napper • Mr. and Mrs. Harold Nash • Juliet Newman • Mr. and Mrs. Frederick C. Norman • Mr. and Mrs. Stanley G. North • Dr. F. S. C. Northrup, Sterling Professor of Philosophy and Law, Yale University • Mrs. Grinnell Noyes • Roderic L. O'Connor • Michele O'Keefe • Mrs. Peter K. Olitsky • Rev. Hendrick M. Osborne • Mrs. Robert Pabst • Raymond Panovec • Bert Parks • Mr. and Mrs. William C. Parrott • Mr. and Mrs. Horace F. Penney • Sydney C. Perell • Lorraine Perry • Mr. and Mrs. Merton Perry • Geraldine Petrizzi • Mr. and Mrs. Louis Petrizzi • Cheryl Pidgursky • Henry H. Pierce, Jr., Union & New Haven Trust Company • Marian Plack • Mr. and Mrs. Chester A. Platt • Mr. and Mrs. Robert L. Polk • Mr. and Mrs. William T. Pooler • Mr. and Mrs. H. Grell Powers • Mr. and Mrs. William W. Prout • Samuel Pryor, Vice-President, Pan-American Airways • Mr. and Mrs. Neil Pultz • Mrs. Carr R. Purser • Juanita Queen • Mrs. Walter Queen • Mr. and Mrs. Thor H. Ramsing • Louise Randolph • Mr. and Mrs. Paul T. Rennell • Dr. and Mrs. Whitman Reynolds, Equitable Life Assurance Society • Mrs. Josephine S. Richardson • Kurt Richardson • John C. Rinello • Mrs. Arthur Roberts • Eleanor Roberts • Chapel Committee, Rosemary Hall, Greenwich • Dr. and Mrs. Harold Rosenberg • Emily H. Roosevelt • Mr. and Mrs. Henry H. Rousseau • Mr. and Mrs. Mr. and Mrs. Henry Rudman • Mrs. Jesse F. Sammis, Jr. • Mrs. Ernest K. Satterlee • Gordon Schmidt, Director, Bruce Museum, Greenwich • Mrs. Henry F. Schwarz • Mr. and Mrs. Eustace Seligman, Sullivan and Cromwell, New York • Mr. and Mrs. Lee Seymour • Marianne Shaw • Mr. and Mrs. John W. Sheppard • Mrs. Grant Simmons • Mr. and Mrs. Langdon B. Simons • Mrs. Merrill R. Smeeth • Dr. and Mrs. Wilson F. Smith • Rev. M. Lawrence Snow, First Methodist Church, Greenwich • Mr. and Mrs. Kenneth Soubry • Mr. and Mrs. Douglas H. Soutar • Mrs. Mary Louise Spang • Mr. and Mrs. G. Hollister Spencer • Mrs. Rubia Spoor • Mrs. Helen Stansbury • Elizabeth Stables • Mrs. Carl Stelling • Mr. and Mrs. Charles L. Stone • Grace Stuttig • George E. Swanson • Mr. and Mrs. John Szanto • Frederick C. Tanner, Jr. • Ann Taylor • Mr. and Mrs. C. Harold Taylor • Juliet Taylor, Miss Porter's School, Farmington • Willard Taylor, Yale Law School • William B. Taylor • Mr. and Mrs. John M. P. Thatcher, Mitchell Hutchins and Co., New York • Rev. Jesse E. Thomas, Round Hill Community Church, Greenwich • Mrs. Frederick B. Vanderbilt

• Mrs. Gerald Vibberts • Dr. and Mrs. John Walker • Thomas J. Watson, Jr., President, International Business Machines • Mr. and Mrs. John R. Webster, Head Master, Greenwich Country Day School • Mr. and Mrs. Clarence L. Welsh • Walter H. Wheeler, Jr., Chairman of the Board, Pitney-Bowes, Inc., Stamford • Rev. C. Lawson Willard, Jr., Trinity Church Episcopal, New Haven • Mr. and Mrs. A. S. R. Williamson • Margery Wilson • Mrs. Alfred C. Wolf • Mrs. C. Martin Wood, Jr. • Mrs. Chase G. Woodhouse, Service Bureau for Women's Organizations • Mrs. George F. Wright • Alois Wyss • Mr. and Mrs. Robert Yoakum

Delaware

Lewis L. Mousley, Jr.

District of Columbia

Regional Head:
Miss Norma Boyd,
1602 Webster St., N.W., Washington, D.C.

John Archbold • His Excellency Aziz Ahmed, Ambassador, Embassy of Pakistan • Joanne Baker • Y. Y. Bao, Ass't. Cultural Attache, Embassy of the Republic of China • Mrs. Walter W. Burleigh • Betty Beale • His Excellency Howard Beale, Ambassador, Embassy of Australia • His Excellency Konan Bedie, Ambassador, Embassy of Ivory Coast Republic • Mr. and Mrs. John M. Begg, "People to People" Program • Dr Mary M. Benyamin • Mrs. Margaret G. Blue • The Honorable Chester Bowles, Special Assistant to the President • Pierre Boyer, Cultural Attache, Embassy of France • Mrs. Frances D. Bryant • A. B. F. Burger, Embassy of the Union of South Africa • Mrs. Walter W. Burleigh • Arthur H. Burling • Mr. and Mrs. Pierre Calogeras, Embassy of Greece • Dr. and Mrs. Warwick Cardozo • Keral Carsen • Mrs. Julia Yates Chandler • Tianethone Chantharasy, Charge d'Affaires, Embassy of Laos • Mrs. Claire L. Chennault • Y. T. Chu, Cultural Attache, Embassy of the Republic of China • His Excellency Il Kwon Chung, Ambassador, Embassy of Korea • Mrs. Janet Claudy • Mrs. Wilda M. Coates • The Honorable John Sherman Cooper, United States Senator from Kentucky • Pauline de Brodes • Finley Peter Dunne, Jr., Director, International Schools Foundation • Mohamed Ali Elsayed, Embassy of United Arab Republic • William H. Feldman • Dr. Robert V. Finley, Director, International Students, Inc. • Mr. and Mrs. William S. Gaud, Ass't Administrator of the New Foreign Agency of the Far East • Alice Glover, Lois-glover Peace Foundation • Rev. Leroy S. Graham, Chaplain, American University • Mrs. Hazel Greene • Elizabeth Grierson • Beulah Hall • Monte Harkins • His Excellency Avraham Harman, Ambassador, Embassy of Israel • Brahim Hayder, Cultural Attache, Embassy of Tunisia • Mrs. J. O. Harmon • Honorable Brooks Hays, Special Assistant to the President • Mary M. Hicks • Beatrice Hicks • Mrs. Jean Hill Dr. Arthur Hummel • Rev. C. C. Hung, Chinese Community Church • Littleton Jackson • Dr. Olov R. T. Janse • Honorable U. Alexis Johnson, Deputy Under-Sec'y. for Political Affairs • His Excellency Dato' Nik Ahmed Kamil, Ambassador, Embassy of the Federation of Malaya • The Honorable Kenneth B. Keating, United States Senator from New York • His Excellency Nong Kimny, Ambassador, Embassy of Cambodia • Willis Kirkland • Simon Kriger, Director, Asian Cultural Exchange Foundation • Dr. P. W. Kuo, Former President, Southeastern University, Republic of China • His Excellency Alexis S. Liatis, Ambassador, Royal Greek Embassy • Dr. Karl E. Lichtenecker, Press Attache, Embassy of Austria • Mrs. A. E. K. Lockwood • His Excellency Jose Antonio Mayobre, Ambassador, Embassy of Venezuela • The Honorable Robert S. McNamara, Secretary of Defense • Nebyam Balakrishna Menon, First Secretary, Embassy of India • Mrs. Myra C. Mobley, Editor, "The Golden Lotus" • Mrs. Blanche S. Moore • Maria Morales • Dr. James M. Nabrit, Jr., President, Howard University • Dr. Ralph A. Newman, School of Law, American University • Thanom Nophawan, Royal Thai Embassy • Ruth Overby • James R. Price, Chief of Washington Bureau, Jami' at al Islam, Inc. • Rilla Q. Pyle • Olga Redman • His Excellency Zenon Rossides, Ambassador, Embassy of Cyprus • His Excellency Guillermo Sevilla Sacasa, Ambassador, Embassy of Nicaragua • Jamal A. Sa'd, Ass't. Director, Arab Information Center • Lester O. Schriver, Former Vice-President, Religious Heritage of America • Mrs. Ruth H. Schwob • His Excellency U. On Sein, Ambassador, Embassy of Burma • L. R. Sethi, Cultural Attache, Embassy of India • Toshiro Shimanouchi, Embassy of Japan • Alice W. Smith • Dr. and Mrs. Laurence C. Staples, Former Exec. Director, All Souls Unitarian Church • Kenneth B. Stephens • Mr. and Mrs. Francis B. Stewart • Blanche Straub • His Excellency Ali Haider Sulaiman, Ambassador, Embassy of Iraq • Elizabeth Sullivan • Frances Sullivan • Louise Sullivan • George Thonseen • George A. Toneman • Colonel S. C. Tong, Representative, Chinese Ministry of Defense • William L. Tsitsiwu, Cultural Attache, Embassy of Ghana • T. L. Tsui, Former Counselor, Embassy of the Republic of China • Charles Wan • Mrs. Andra Weaver • Mr. and Mrs. H. B. Weiss • Hazel Wharton • G. D. L. White, Charge d'Affaires, Embassy of New Zealand • Andrew Wicketts • Mrs. Sadie Williams • Alfred Wimer • The Honorable Robert F. Woodward, Ass't. Secretary, Department of State • Assayed Ahmad Ali Zabarah, Charge d'Affaires, Embassy of Yemen • His Excellency Ardashir Zahedi, Ambassador, Embassy of Iran

Florida

Beverly Barnes • Elizabeth Barnes • Lawrence R. Boyer • Mrs. Manuel Bromberg • Colonel O. E. Davis • Mrs. Ethel J. Dow • Bryan Dusseault • Rev. Marie Ellis, Church of Religious Science, Jacksonville • Mrs. John P. Feaster • Samuel Friedland • Mrs. Ann Georgia • Dr. Henry James, Unitarian Fellowship • Mrs. Alexandra Landis • Ginny Millay • Raymond S. Miller • Rev. and Mrs. M. McBride Panton, Church of Spiritual Philosophy, St. Petersburg • Swami Parampanthi • Alberta E. Reeser • Ralph Roberts • Rose Spencer • Roman Stanley • Witgen Stein • Mrs. Alex Stuart • Dorris Witgenstein • LeRoy Zemke

Georgia

Harllee Branch, Jr., President, The Southern Company, Atlanta • Mrs. Vera F. Moore • Mrs. Annette Vincent

Hawaii

Regional Heads:
Mr. and Mrs. William A. Shimer,
Maunaolu College,
Paia, Maui, Hawaii

Mrs. Walter Dillingham • Jacob Feuerring • Dr. Charles A. Moore, Senior Professor of Philosophy, University of Hawaii • Mr. and Mrs. William A. Shimer, Maunaolu College • Gregg M. Sinclair • Murray Turnbull, Chairman, East-West Center Committee, University of Hawaii • Mrs. Roy. A. Vitousek • Dr. Willard Wilson, Vice-President, University of Hawaii

Illinois

Regional Head:
Miss Ethel Wells Smalley,
400 West Deming Place, Chicago 14, Illinois

Mr. and Mrs. John W. Baer • Harry Barnard • Mrs. Hilbert Bengston • Rev. Russell Bietzer, North Shore Unitarian Church • Mrs. Emil C. Blocks • Dr. Preston Bradley, The People's Church of Chicago • Mrs. Horace A. Brogan • Martha Brown • Mrs. Elizabeth Caruso • Edmond M. Cook, President, John Deere Foundation • Maggie Daly • Mr. and Mrs. Edmund J. Doering, II • William J. Donnelly, Jr., Northwestern University • Mrs. Charles W. Dotson • Louis Duman • Rev. John Evans • Mr. and Mrs. Cola A. Gray • Julia Hodge • Lee Howard • Mrs. George R. Jones • Mrs. Howard L. Jones • Mr. and Mrs. R. Bruce McManus • Jean Peterson • Mrs. Ruth K. Schacherer • Dr. John Sheinen • Dr. Henry A. Smith, President, The Theosophical Society of America • Mr. and Mrs. William E. Van Winkle • Mrs. Gordon Ware • Dorothy Weaver • Mrs. Julia Proctor White

Indiana

Elizabeth Bridwell • Walter Brigadier, Earlham College • L. L. Castetter • Mrs. A. Barry Ellis • Mrs. Stephen Kurtz • Jane Blaffer Owen

Iowa

Dr. Marcus Bach, School of Religion, University of Iowa • Mrs. Marion Downing • Lee Gilbert • Mrs. Gerald Levy • Mrs. James W. Wallace

Kansas

Regional Head:
Miss Louise Kieninger,
1149 Washburn St., Topeka, Kansas

Lois English • Mrs. R. N. Ewing • Ruth Hulsey • Verna Moyer Shirley Reed • Gyaneshwar Singh, University of Wichita • Mrs. Norma Statton • Larry Tijerina

Kentucky

Elizabeth M. Cosby • Edith Markley • Mrs. Kenneth H. Thompson • Gil Wilson

Louisianna

Mrs. Anna Bickseer • Mrs. W. H. Faurote • Mrs. Anita P. Frossard • Mrs. George J. Wilt, Sr.

Maine

Mary W. Dewson • Mrs. Sydney Greenbie • Mrs. P. E. Hitchcock • Peter S. Wilson

Maryland

Regional Head:
Mrs. John Baldwin
1302 John St., Baltimore, Md.

Nicholas L. Andris • Mrs. C. Victor Barry • Mr. and Mrs. John M. Begg • Gordon F. Boardman • Mrs. Alice Braemer • Eileen Canterbury • Mr. and Mrs. Gordon Chapman • C. C. Chen • Mr. and Mrs. Corwith Cramer, Jr. • Mrs. Lillian S. Dembrow • F. Millard Foard • Mr. and Mrs. Stephen Gansbaro • Mr. and Mrs. Harold Ganss, Sr. • Mr. and Mrs. Harold Ganss, Jr. • Mrs. James V. Goure • Mrs. Leland A. Graham • Margaret Hanson Eunice Hoffman • Priscilla Howard • Mr. and Mrs. Michael Jasperson • Richard L. Jen • Margaret Johnson • Delar Kimble • Dr. Y. C. Koo, International Monetary Fund • Wunsz King • Dr. Otto F. Kraushaar, President, Goucher College • Florence E. Landon • Mrs. Marrion Larkin • Mr. and Mrs. Louis Liljedahl • Jerry Martin • Mrs. D. Grant Mickle • H. E. Mohammed Nemazee • Mr. and Mrs. Henry E. Niles • Mrs. Roland Perusse • Harry S. Plager • Mrs. Marion Potter • Edward N. Rich, Jr. Mr. and Mrs. Robert L. Rich • Mr. and Mrs. Woodward S. Rich • Eugene O. Saphir • H. M. Schwarzchild • Malcolm C. Spensley • The Honorable J. Millard Tawes, Governor, State of Maryland • Lewis Theon • Jeanette Vestraci • Mrs. Success Vestraci • Mrs. Albert G. Warfield • Mrs. Elizabeth Weaver • Dr. Richard Weigle, President, St. John's College • Dr. and Mrs. John Whitridge • Mr. and Mrs. William Zens

Massachusetts

Regional Head:
Mrs. Roger Hallowell
585 Gay St., Westwood, Mass.

R. Aube • Mrs. Samuel L. Batcheldor • Rev. Daniel Bliss, The American Board of Commissioners for Foreign Missions • Mrs. Luther A. Breck, Sr. • Mrs. William M. Carson • Mrs. Harold C. Case • Grace C. Cederberg • Dr. and Mrs. Robert Dumm, Dean, Boston Conservatory of Music • Dr. Deane W. Ferm, Dean of the Chapel, Mt. Holyoke College • Marie Foskett • The Honorable Foster Furcolo, Former Governor, State of Massachusetts • Philip Randall Giles, General Superintendent, Universalist Church of America • Rabbi Roland B. Gittelsohn, Temple Israel, Boston • Mrs. Livingston Hall, Head Mistress, Concord Academy • Mr. and Mrs. Kessle • Rev. Ernest W. Kuebler • William G. Laurans, President, Laurans Bros. • James Lawrence, Jr. • Herbert Marks • Joseph Marzullo, Jr., Dean College, Franklin • Kirtley Mather, Geologic Museum, Cambridge • Kodo Matsunami, Center for the Study of World Religions at Harvard University • James F. McGuire • L. H. S. Osae-Addo, Harvard University • William Pike • Lawson Prince, Concord Academy • Beatrix Rumford, Wellesley College • Mrs. Phillip J. Rulon • Mrs. Eloise C. Simpson • Mary Ann Skruta • Dr. Huston Smith, Professor of Philosophy, Massachusetts Institute of Technology • Mrs. Philip B. Terry • Mrs. Margaret Thurston, Wellesley College • Joseph Venti • John Werby • Mr. and Mrs. J. Howland Wilson • Sao H. H. Win, Center for the Study of World Religions at Harvard University • Mr. and Mrs. David B. Wray

Michigan

Regional Head:

Miss Cora Palmer
5992 Hillcrest, Detroit 36, Mich.

American Grail Foundation • Mrs. Dorothy D. Bawiec • Mrs. Anthony Bonadio • Ned A. Brodbeck • Claud Carver • Robert Carver Carrie B. Cooper • Mrs. Margaret D. Cooper • S. T. Elder • • B. Follette • Bertha Harmon • Richard Harvey • Mr. and Mrs. Charles Holtsberry • Kaye C. Holtsberry • M. P. Jennings • Mrs. Mary Hines King • Don Knight • Ivan Konkel • W. L. Lewis • Peggy Maxwell • Frank L. Oktavec • Mrs. Donald T. Owen • Mr. and Mrs. D. W. Palmer • Rev. David F. Pittman, First Baptist Church, Dearborn • Theodor Pong • Dr. A. Rossetti • Mrs. Ira Spieker • Floyd Starr, Starr Commonwealth for Boys • Gregg E. Stover • Mrs. Leonard M. Stuttman • Mary Swartout • Mr. and Mrs. Clyde Trepanier • J. A. Vander Werf • R. E. Van Hoosear • Minoru Yamasaki • Ralph G. Zirkle

Minnesota

Oscar Dahl • Rev. Sidney W. Goldsmith, Jr. Shattuck Shool, Raribault • John Jefferson Olney

Mississippi

Mrs. Harry M. Ashcraft • Mrs. Ernest L. Jahncke, Sr.

Missouri

Regional Head:
Miss Elizabeth Gempp
9227 Sappington Road, St. Louis, Mo.

Mrs. Ora M. Bura • Richard L. Carp • Mrs. Pete Cherry • Mrs. E. V. Cowdry • Mrs. T. F. Croskey • Rev. Elsom Eldridge, Head of Educational Center, The Episcopal Diocese of Missouri • Mrs. A. T. Esslinger • Mr. and Mrs. Donald Grant • Mrs. Floyd C. Klein • Christine Love • Mrs. Edward K. Love, Jr. • W. R. Persons, President, The Emerson Electric Mfg. Co. • Mr. and Mrs. Paul Rava • Mr. and Mrs. Bob Roberts • Swami Satprakashananda, The Vedanta Society • Mrs. Robert Starbird, Former Dean of Women, Washington University • Taka May Campfire Girls

Montana

Mrs. Robert C. Line • Mr. and Mrs. W. D. Miller • Henry Potter

Nebraska

Regional Head:
Mrs. Mary Elaine Hall
120 South 90th St., Omaha, Neb.

Mr. and Mrs. Ora W. Carrell • Mr. and Mrs. John F. Davis • Mr. and Mrs. Philip Dodge • Jane Ely

New Hampshire

Dr. Wing-Tsit Chan, Professor of Chinese Culture and Philosophy, Dartmouth College • Douglas Horton • Eva F. Hunt • Mr. and Mrs. John B. Morton • Marquise Dedons de Pierrefeu • Douglas Sloan, "Cathedral In The Pines"

New Jersey

Elizabeth C. Allen • Philip H. Ashby • Mrs. Elsa F. R. Bartke • Mrs. G. R. Beck • Mrs. Betty Bell • Emily S. Brown • Mr. and Mrs. Harry A. Burgess • Mrs. Irene Burrell • Mrs. Virginia B. Caputo • Mr. and Mrs. B. William Dudley • Fellowship of Divine Truth • Mrs. William G. Finigan • Dr. Anges N. Flack • Mrs. Mildred Fletcher • Mrs. Gertrude Garda • Mrs. W. J. Gassert • Dr. and Mrs. Francis R. B. Godolphin, Princeton University • Mr. and Mrs. William G. Goldenberg • Dr. Ernest Gordon, Dean of the Chapel, Princeton University • Dr. and Mrs. Arthur Harper • Mrs. James M. Harrison • T. Victor Hart • Rev. Marguerite Iwerson, First Church of Religious Science, Plainfield • Mrs. Harriette F. Jacobs • Mrs. Harry Kilminster • Mrs. Maulsby Kimball • Mrs. Joseph Kolodny • Mrs. A. R. Lamb, Jr. • E. D. LaRue • Mrs. William F. Leach • Corinne Levin • Mrs. Robert F. Longacre • Dorothea Malcom • The Honorable Robert B. Meyner, Former Governor, State of New Jersey • Mr. and Mrs. Clinton E. Mosher • Rev. Rowland Nye • Sally Oliver • Dr. Robert B. Pinerman • Mrs. Eben Powell • Mrs. R. W. Purdy • Lt. Commander and Mrs. Nathaniel Ratner • Mr. and Mrs. Hans Schaeffer • Mrs. Eric Steiner • Mrs. Edith Stiles • Mrs. Gladys Stockton • Mrs. W. H. Tidd • Dr. and Mrs. Joseph Videtti • Mrs. Mabel Wain • Mrs. Ernest Zaisser

New Mexico

Thomas D. Campbell • Dr. and Mrs. Francis Merchant

New York

Regional Head:
Mrs. Garret J. Garretson
105 East 22nd St., New York, N. Y.

Michael Adrian • Mrs. Timothy F. Allen • Arab Students in the U.S.A., Organization of • Maria Arnold • Dr. Max Arzt, Jewish Theological Seminary of America • Takeshi Asada • Mr. and Mrs. H. R. Ashton • Hugh D. Auchincloss, Jr., International Development Assn. • Daniel L. Baker • Barney Balaban, President, Paramount Pictures Corporation • Mr. and Mrs. William H. Baldwin • Rev. Raymond C. Barker, First Church of Religious Science, New York • Mrs. L. Barnes • Mrs. Luther G. Battin • Mrs. Joanne Baxter • Mr. and Mrs. Don V. Becker • Mr. Beezarde Rev. Lee H. Bell, Exec. Secretary, The Methodist Federation for Social Action • Mrs. Rose Bell • His Excellency Armand Berard, Ambassador of France to the United Nations • Jack Bernstein • Sanford C. Bernstein • Pauline Bielemier • Mrs. Devee B. Bingham • Rev. Joseph P. Bishop, The Presbyterian Church, Rye • His Excellency D. S. Bitsios, Ambassador of Greece to the United Nations • Dr. Walter E. Bock, St. Peter's Lutheran Church of Manhattan • Mr. and Mrs. L. C. Bohs • Mrs. Allan Bond • Mrs. Sterling Boos • Gardiner L. Boothe, Jr., Rushton, Peabody and Associates • Mrs. Francis T. Boyd • Mrs. Frank Breeze • Florence Brobeck • Susan Bromberg, Barnard College • Mr. and Mrs. Harold W. Brown • James Oliver Brown • Dr. and Mrs. Robert T. Browne • Mr. and Mrs. Earl J. Brubaker • Marya Bryant • Mrs. Winthrop Buck • Mrs. Thomas F. Bundy • Dr. and Mrs. Henry T. Burns • Mrs. William G. Burns • Dr. E. A. Burtt, Cornell University • Mr. and Mrs. Chester F. Carlson • Mrs. D. Carter • Ruth Chalmers, Exec. Director, Jane Addams Peace Association • Leigh Chamberlain • Lillian Chambers • His Excellency Sisouk Na Champassak, Ambassador of Laos to the United Nations • Mike Claman • Mrs. Ruth Gage Colby • His Excellency Gershon Collier, Ambassador of Sierra Leone to the United Nations • Dr. J. C. Collins • Mrs. Joan Collins • Mrs. Rose Comito • Mrs. William C. Conner • Benjamin Cooper • Arthur P. Crabtree, Supervisor of Adult Education, University of the State of New York • Dr. Louis J. Crane • Robert Leland Crowell, President Thomas Y. Crowell Company, New York • Richard Darsney • Rabbi Charles Davidson, Temple Emanu-el, New York • Elizabeth G. Davis • S. A. Diell • Edward Dilday • Rev. and Mrs. Lowell Russell Ditzen, The Reformed Church, Bronxville • Mrs. Marie Dobrecky • The Rt. Rev. Horace W. B. Donegan, Bishop, Diocese of New York • Mr. and Mrs. J. W. Donner • Mr. and Mrs. William F. Dornbusch • Mrs. Davis T. Dunbar, Sr. • David Durst • Edna Eckert • Mr. and Mrs. Orville D. Edwards • Rabbi Maurice N. Eisendrath, President, Union of American Hebrew Congregations • Colonel J. R. Elyachar • Hilda Cole Espy • Raymond Ewell • Mr. and Mrs. Stephen J. Feit • Mrs. Mary D. Feldman • Harry A. Feldman • Rabbi Louis Finkelstein, Jewish Theological Seminary of America • H. F. Fischbach • Mrs. Welthy Fisher, President, World Education, Inc. • Jack Fishberg • Mrs. Richard W. Flader • Simone France • Mrs. E. Frank • Hubert French • Mrs. J. G. Friedman • Mrs. Sidney Friedman • Charles Frost • Vincent Gabriel • Roland Gammon, Former Director, Laymen's Movement, World Parliament of Religions • Madame Giuseppe Garibaldi • Lyn Gaylord • Miss Grace Gearity • Mrs. Francis H. Geer • Mrs. Walter Gibbs • Hermione Gingold • Dorothy Glazer • Gertrude Glazer • Rev. William Glenesk, Spencer Memorial Church, Brooklyn Heights • Arthur Godfrey • Rabbi David Golovensky, Temple Beth-El, New Rochelle • Rabbi Samuel H. Gordon, Community Synagogue, Rye • Bruce Graham • Dr. Frank Graham, United Nations Representative for India and Pakistan • Kay Rainey Gray • Mr. and Mrs. Thomas Marshall Green • Dr. Louis M. Hacker, Professor of Economics, Columbia University • Mrs. Alexander Hamilton • Inga Hang • Welles Hangen, N.B.C. News • Rev. Donald S. Harrington, Community Church of New York • Mrs. Leroy B. Harris • Leroy W. Harris, Sr. • Michael G. Harris, Harriman, Ripley & Co. • Mrs. John T. Harrison, Jr., Board of Directors of the Y.W.C.A. of the City of New York • John T. Harrison Jr., Flynn, Harrison and Conroy, New York • Patricia Harvey • Dr. Saadat Hasan, Arab States Delegations • Mrs. Russell Hauser • Mr. and Mrs. John Hay • Mr. and Mrs. Henry Helm • Marie Henderson • Mrs. Reilda Henderson • Anna M. Heyen • William Hirscher • Mr. and Mrs. Fred Hobby • Ernest Hodossy • Margaret Hoel • Mr. and Mrs. Sherman Holman • Mayme V. Holmes • Evalina V. Honsinger • Mrs. Frederick S. Hoppin • Mr. and Mrs. Robert Houk • John Howland, President, Woodward, Baldwin and Company • Dr. Elizabeth Hubbard • Mrs. Roger B. Hull • Richard D. Ince, G. C. Haas and Company • Wallace Irwin, Director of Public Services, United States Mission to the United Nations • Mr. and Mrs. Horace Isleib • Mrs. Paul L. Kohns • Mrs. Olga Jackson • Mrs. John H. Jackson • Mrs. Nicholas Jacobus • Dr. Martha Jaeger, Chairman, Friends' Conference on Religion and Psychology • Herman Jaffe • Mr. and Mrs. Theodore R. Jarvis • His Excellency C. S. Jha, Embassy of India, Ottawa, Canada • Mrs. Constance L. Jessop • R. E. Julien • Mrs. Annaliese Karl • Regina Keller • James Crain Kellogg, III, Vice-Chairman, Port of New York Authority • Rabbi Rabbi Morris N. Kertzer, Larchmont Temple • Mrs. Kilmer • Mrs. Stockton Kimball • Mrs. Wilbur Kirwan • Simon Klein • Mrs. Harry S. Knabel • Edgar M. Kneedler • Brewster Kneen, Fellowship of Reconciliation • Mrs. Leo Kornfeld • Harold Kron • Mr. and Mrs. F. L. Kunz, Director Foundation for Integrated Education, Inc. • Dr. John Kunz • Dr. Robert W. Laidlaw, Chief of Psychiatric Services, Roosevelt Hospital, New York Mr. and Mrs. Charles R. Langmuir • Mrs. Lavid • Walter S. Lemmon, World Wide Broadcasting Foundation, Inc. • Max Lerner, New York Post • Mr. and Mrs. Leonard E. LeSourd, Exec. Editor, "Guideposts" • Mrs. Allyn Ley • James Linen, President, Time, Life, Inc., New York • Mrs. Martha Linn • Philip S. Linnik, Director, Universal Brotherhood Center • Mrs. Emil Lipke • Mrs. G. E. Logan • Mrs. Carol Lord • Mr. and Mrs. Robert F. Loree, Jr. • Wendy Alix Loree • Mrs. Robert Lorenz • John MacElroy • Mr. and Mrs. George Mack • C. H. MacLachlan • Mr. and Mrs. Daniel E. MacLean • August Maffray, Treasurer, Asia Society, Inc. • Mrs. Ella Magyar • Robert H. Malcolm • Victoria Moore, Vassar College • Sanford Malter • Mr. and Mrs. Theodore L. Mander • Dora Marcus • Rabbi Israel Margolies, Beth Am, The People's Temple, New York • Rabbi Julius Mark, Temple Emanu-El, New York • Mr. and Mrs. Murray Martin • Bess Massarsky • Armen Matassiori • Edouard D'A. Mathiotte • Carola Goya and Matteo • Mrs. Gordon McCulloh • Mr. and Mrs. Toivo J. Merikaarto • Daisy Meyer • Rabbi Irving Miller, American Zionist Council • Valerie Miller • Garry Moore • Mrs. Barbara Morgan • Amanda Mortimer • Elizabeth Mower • Clyde B. Morgan, President, Rayonier, Inc. • Mildred Motley • Milton Mumford, President, Lever Brothers, New York • Buell Mullen • T. J. Natarajan, Sec'y., Advisory Committee on Administrative and Budgetary Questions at the United Nations • Dr. Reuben S. Nathan, Policy Director, "Radio Free Europe" • Mrs. J. E. Nelson • Robert Neubeck • Mrs. Elsie S. Newman • Mrs. William B. Nichols • Dr. Margaret Nordfeldt • Theodore Okie, President, J. W. Mathes, Inc., New York • His Excellency Katsuo Okazaki, Ambassador of Japan to the United Nations • Mr. and Mrs. George Olden, Batten, Barton, Durstine & Osborn, Inc., New York • Mrs. Samuel G. Ordway • Mr. and Mrs. John Orr • Catharine A. Parsell • Swami Pavitrananda, Vedanta Society of New York • Mrs. Charles S. Perry • Mrs. Phillipps • Mrs. Virginia V. Phillipps • Mrs. Helen Post • Mr. and Mrs. Nicholas Post • Tony, Cora and Elaine Prantner • Dr. Ira Progoff, Foundation for Integral Research • Mr. and Mrs. Edmund Pugh • His Excellency Kamel A. Rahim, Ambassador, Permanent Delegation of the League of Arab States to the United Nations • Mrs. Ogden R. Reid • Mrs. Walker Reid • Eleanor Ribera • Dr. A. Rieger • Mrs. Rimbach • Cliff S. C. Robertson • Jackie Robinson • Rev. James Robinson, Church of the Master, New York • Joel Robnson • John D. Rockefeller, IV • Dr. Ida Rolf • Henry F. Rollman • David Rose • Mrs. Elizabeth Rose • Mr. and Mrs. Julius Rosenberg • Mr. and Mrs. Melvin Ross • Clinton Rossiter, Dep't. of Government, Cornell University • Thomas Rothfield •

Rudivoravan, Princess of Thailand • Mrs. Mollie Rutkove • A. Rypp • Ruth St. Denis • Richard Salant, President, C.B.S. News, New York • Joseph Samuels • Ezra Schmid • Mrs. Michael M. Schwab • Mr. and Mrs. John Schweitzer • Dr. Ervin Seale, Church of the Truth, New York • Sidney Z. Searles, President, Interfaith Movement, Inc. • Mr. and Mrs. Maurice Sellers • Mr. and Mrs. E. B. Sellon • Mrs. Charlton Shell • Mrs. Leonard Sherman • Mrs. H. F. Silver • Mr. and Mrs. Wellington Simpson • W. J. Sloss, Marron, Sloss & Co., Inc. • Mrs. C. A. Smith, • Mrs. Mary Smith • Shirley B. Smith, Director, Women's Africa Committee, New York • Dr. Ralph W. Sockman, Christ Church, New York • Loraine Sterling • Clement F. Stigdon, Jr. • B. F. Stolinsky • Mrs. Robert Morgan Stopford • Alma Strassner • Anna Lord Strauss • Elsie Sweet, Barnard College • Jean Tabaud • Elizabeth A. Tainan • Rabbi Marc H. Tannenbaum, Institute of Human Relations, The American Jewish Committee • Alix Taylor • Mr. and Mrs. Matt Taylor • John Terken • Walter N. Thayer, President, New York Herald Tribune • Mabel I. Thomas • Norman Thomas, Director Emeritus, Civil Liberties Union • Mrs. Leslie K. Thompson • Janet Tillman • Francesca Turi, Sarah Lawrence College • Colonel Alden Twachtman • United Lodge of Theosophists, New York • Hector Uvertall • H. E. Mehdi Vakil • Dr. Henry Pitt Van Dusen, President, Union Theological Seminary, New York • Rev. John Van Zanten, Riverdale Presbyterian Church • Vincent J. J. Vigouraux • Mrs. Charles Von Glahn • Rev. Henry J. Wahl, Second Reformed Church of Flatbush • Mr. and Mrs. Forrest Walker • Dorothy Wallace • Mrs. Henry G. Walter • Dr. Charles L. Warren, St. Mark's Church, New York • Mr. and Mrs. Edward S. Watts • Norma Weast • Mr. and Mrs. Paul Weast • Mrs. A. P. Webber • Mr. and Mrs. George Weber • Norman Weis • Clara Weiss • Ray West Rev. Moran Weston, St. Philip's Church, New York • Mrs. Bruce Whitmore • Mr. and Mrs. John Eric Wideberg • Mrs. Herbert M. Wilkinson • Theresa Wilkosz • "Bill Wilson" • Mr. and Mrs. Henry Winchester • Nellie E. Wing • Frederick M. Winship, United Press International, New York • Mrs. Harold Winthrop • Mrs. Henry W. Wittinger • Clement J. Wyle • Mrs. F. Yankowitz • Madame Antonina Yassukovitch • Marianne Zadroshy • Austin Zender

North Carolina

Mrs. Lola M. Hawkland • Salvatore Rapisardi, Duke University • Dr. J. B. Rhine, Duke University • Dr. Sullivan, Department of Religion, Duke University

North Dakota

Mrs. Ray Beyer • Mrs. Albert Bowman • Mrs. Fred Dahl • Mrs. Bella Foust • Mrs. Lillian Johnson • Mrs. Harland Long • Mrs. Frieda Monson • Mrs. Frank Nester • Mrs. Emma Perrin • Mrs. Ray Putney • Mrs. Kenneth Sletto

Ohio

Mrs. Timothy Ackley • Rev. Benjamin H. Clark • Hilda B. Cones • Mrs. Margaret Dean • Mrs. William H. Dockus • Mrs. Cyrus .. Eaton • Martin Fiege • Dr. Nelson Glueck, President, Hebrew Union College — Jewish Institute of Religion, Cincinnati • Louise Hume • Mrs. Nola Jones • Mr. and Mrs. Robert Kaltenback • Kenneth J. Lea • Mrs. Harvey C. Lisle • Mr. and Mrs. James Long • Mrs. John MacGurie • David May, Kenyon College, Gambier • Mrs. J. Ray Miller • Mr. and Mrs. H. S. Patterson • Patty Rons • Mrs. Lillian Smith • Mr. and Mrs. Charles Taylor • Mr. and Mrs. Walter A. Taylor • Rev. Grover Thornsberry, Unity Center of Practical Christianity • Mrs. C. A. Thum • Mrs. Volney Traxler • Dr. A. Ashley Weech, Professor of Pediatrics, University of Cincinnati • Mrs. A. Ashley Weech

Oklahoma

The Honorable J. Howard Edmondson, Governor, State of Oklahoma

Oregon

Ruth C. Babb • Mrs. M. J. Coleman • Mr. and Mrs. A. A. McCormack • Mr. and Mrs. Harry E. Vogtman

Pennsylvania

Regional Heads:
Mr. and Mrs. Maurice M. Rosen
303 Ingeborge Road, Philadelphia 51, Penna.

James Abrams, Franklin & Marshall College, Lancaster • Clara C. S. Perôt d'Amply • Gustave G. Amsterdam, Chairman and President, Bankers Securities Corp., Philadelphia • Mr. and Mrs. Robert Andrews • Mrs. Katharine Arnett • Helen Bailey • S. H. Ballam, Jr. • Frank Binswanger, Jr., Binswanger Corporation, Philadelphia • Mrs. Robert E. Blanc • Jack Blumenfeld • Mrs. Garrett D. Bowne, Jr. • John Boyd • Pearl Buck • Burke • Mrs. Stuart Caine • Jack A. Cannon • Lucy Perkens Carner • Blumenfeld • Mrs. Garrett D. Bowne, Jr. • John Boyd • Pearl Buck Richard S. Burgess, Friends' Central School, Philadelphia • Mrs. Lillian Burke • Mrs. Stuart Caine • Jack A. Cannon • Lucy Perkens Carner Martin Casper • Miriam Cone • John F. Connelly, Crown Cork & Seal Company, Philadelphia • Mrs. Edna L. Cowan • Geoffrey J. Cunniff • Mr. and Mrs. Robert H. Cunningham • Samuel H. Daroff, H. Daroff & Sons, Philadelphia • William L. Day, Chairman of the Board, The First Pennsylvania Banking & Trust Co., Philadelphia • Dr. Margaret N. Dealy • Martin M. Decker, The Decker Corporation, Bala Cynwyd • Mrs. Davis T. Dunbar, Jr. • Selden Dunbar • Kanak Dutta • Mrs. Frances Ekey • Mrs. Janet W. Elinsky • Rebecca P. Elliott • Mrs. Mary Emily Pollock Ellis • G. F. Emerson, Friends' Central School, Philadelphia • Marty Emerson • Milton C. Endres • Mrs. Charles Evoy • Mrs. Herman Feldman • William F. Fischer, Jr. • Edward L. Frankel • Vincent E. Furey, Girard Trust Corn Exchange Bank, Philadelphia • Z. H. Garfield • Matthew Giuffrida, Field Representative, American Baptist Home Mission Societies • Mrs. Jonas B. Goldman • Mrs. Edward Gordon • Mrs. Edward Grainer • Dr. Frederick R. Griffin • Mrs. Frederick R. Griffin, Jr. • Edna Hale • Joseph J. Harris, West Philadelphia Federal Savings & Loan Ass'n. • Mathilde Harrison • Mr. and Mrs. Abram Haupt • Mr. and Mrs. Irwin Haupt • Mrs. Max Haupt • Heller & Rosen • James Hill, Hill-Chase & Co., Inc., Philadelphia • Lawrence Horowitz, Young Adjustment Co., Philadelphia • Vaughn R. Jackson, First Pennsylvania Banking & Trust Co., Philadelphia • Mrs. Edward Morris Jones • J. Harrison Jones, Broad Street Trust Company, Philadelphia • Mr. and Mrs. Milton A. Kamsler • Mrs. David Kanter • Mrs. N. J. Kaplan • Mrs. A. Karoe • Lawrence Katz • Henry Kaufman, Rosenthal & Kaufman, Merion • Mrs. Albert Kerster • Samuel Laver • W. J. Leslie • Abraham Levin • Mr. and Mrs. Paul Longnecker • Ralph K. Madway, Main Line Homes, Inc., Wayne • Albert T. Mason, President, Liberty Real Estate Bank & Trust Co., Philadelphia • Louise Mattlage • Thomas W. McConkey • William J. Meinel, Heintz M'fg. Company, Philadelphia • Mrs. F. A. Mitsch • Mrs. Myra C. Mobley • Mrs. Nathan Molodow • Mrs. Frederick W. Muller, Jr. • Dr. and Mrs. Oscar S. Nelson • Mrs. Thornton Oakley • Rev. Samuel S. Odom, St. Stephen's Episcopal Church, Sewickley • Jose de Pedroso, Marques de San Carlos de Pedroso • Eleanor Pollock, Women's Editor, "Evening and Sunday Bulletin" • Lee Purser, The Shipley School, Bryn Mawr • Augustus L. Raffetto, Philadelphia National Bank, Philaderphia • Mrs. E. L. Rimer • Mrs. Abram E. Ritt • Mr. and Mrs. John Roger, Editor, "The Golden Lotus" • G. E. Rosenau, Rosenau Bros., Inc., Philadelphia • Arthur Rosenberg, Food Fair Stores, Inc., Philadelphia • Bernard H. Sandman, Jr. • Sol Satinsky, Franford Woolen Mills, Philadelphia • Mr. and Mrs. Douglas R. Schoenfeld, Insurance Co. of North America, Devon • Dr. Philip B. Secor, Director of Religious Life, Dickenson College, Carlisle • E. Victor Seixas, Jr. • Lauren Joan Simon • Marie Sloan • Mrs. Ann Webb Snyder • J. F. Specht • Mrs. Clarence Stern • Ruth Stewart • John Syz, Business School, University of Pennsylvania • Mrs. A. K. Waldron • Hedy Wassmer • Matthew Weinstein • William Morton West • Irving B. Waxlar • Mr. and Mrs. Alexander B. Wheeler • D. Robert Yarnall, Jr. • Bruce Yoskin, Friends Central School, Philadelphia • Mr. and Mrs. Harold Yoskin • Mrs. Irwin C. Young

Rhode Island

Mrs. Lionel Lewis • John B. McConaughea

South Dakota

Mrs. R. M. Whitney

Texas

Regional Head:
Mrs. Elizabeth May
4806 Merrimac St., Corpus Christi, Texas

Mrs. Helen Adele • Mrs. Jack Anderson • Mrs. Florence Barry • Mrs. Bert Bowman • Mrs. H. A. Emig • Mr. and Mrs. Lloyd Fulke • Mrs. Paul A. Gerard • Rev. Alfred Henriksen • Dr. Frank Hovell • Ernest J. Larson • Dr. and Mrs. Mark Pomerantz • Dr. and Mrs. Alfred Taylor, Research Scientist, Biochemical Institute, University of Texas • Harlan Taylor • Mrs. June Teter • Mrs. Phillip Wallock

Utah

Mr. and Mrs. Henry C. Flesher, "New Age Expositor" • Elaine S. Michelsen

Vermont

Mrs. Lucille Banford • Former Ambassador and Mrs. Ellsworth Bunker • Mr. and Mrs. John Burdett • Jane Mitchell • Mr. and Mrs. Richard Steele

Virginia

Mrs. Rae E. Allen • Mrs. Joseph Bragdon • Mrs. Carl S. Clancy • George K. Hundley • Fred Jordan, Internat'l. General Assembly of Spiritualists • Rear Admiral and Mrs. Lee • Harold R. Levy, Internat'l. General Assembly of Spiritualists • Mrs. John S. Martin, Sr. • Adele Michael • Margaret Morris • Mr. and Mrs. Albert Nelison, BMI • Mrs. Preston Parish • Mrs. Ruth Starr Rose • Mrs. E. C. Sherry • Mrs. J. T. Singleton • Annie Trussell • Bonnie Trussell • Mrs. T. E. Turner, Jr. • Jerry Van Voorhis, College of William and Mary

Washington

Mrs. J. O. Harmon • Mrs. Gertrude K. Haven • Mrs. Roger Jenkins • Karen Lindner • Swami Vividishananda, Ramakrishna Vedanta Center, Seattle

West Virginia

Art Campbell • Karl Wachs

Wisconsin

Mrs. Edward Arndt • Mrs. Catherine Arnold • Harry Banzhaf • Barbara Breske • Carol A. Frakes • Joseph I. Taylor • Irene Thomas

Wyoming

C. C. Scott, Jr.

Venezuela

Professor E. George

The foregoing list of sponsors is complete as of date of printing, but does not include names of sponsors received subsequent to this date.

INDEX OF INDIVIDUALS *

*Sponsors and officers of Temple of Understanding not included unless in text.

I

J

K

L

M

N

O

P

GENERAL INDEX

B

C

D

E

F

G

H

I

J

K

L

M

N

O

P

Q

R

S

T

U

V

W

Y

Z

THE TEMPLE OF UNDERSTANDING

www.ingramcontent.com/pod-product-compliance
Lightning Source LLC
Chambersburg PA
CBHW052106270326
41931CB00012B/2912

* 9 7 8 2 9 2 5 3 6 9 6 5 3 *